Hitchhiking the World

Hitchhiking the World

Through 132 Countries

50 Adventures

by Kevin McNally

Edited by Stacy Radford & Heidi Lewis

Taj Mahal Press

Suzanne & "Dennis"

Happy Holidays!

Heidi

12/2016

In memory of
Sue, Carolyn, and Ben

Library of Congress Cataloging-in-Publication Data

McNally, Kevin
Hitchhiking the World: Through 132 Countries 50 Adventures /
Kevin McNally – First paperback edition.
pages 238; 15.24 x 22.86 cm
ISBN-13: 978-1492864714
ISBN-10: 1492864714
BISAC: Travel / Essays & Travelogues

This book is dedicated to planet earth for providing a beautiful place to explore and to all of the people who get it and give it. Shine on!

Everything you want is on the other side of fear.

"Be yourself. Everyone else is taken." Maggie in Amsterdam

Traveler's Prayer

Grant me the ability, Great Spirit,
to see the beauty in unexpected places,
the talent in unexpected people,
and the grace to tell them so.

The Guest House
Rumi, 13ᵗʰ Century Poet

This being human is a guest house.
Every morning a new arrival.
A joy, a depression, a meanness,
some momentary awareness comes
as an unexpected visitor.
Welcome and entertain them all!
Even if they are a crowd of sorrows,
who violently sweep your house
empty of its furniture,
still treat each guest honorably.
He may be clearing you out for some new delight.
The dark thought, the shame, the malice,
meet them at the door laughing,
and invite them in.
Be grateful for whoever comes,
because each has been sent
as a guide from beyond.

Continents of the World

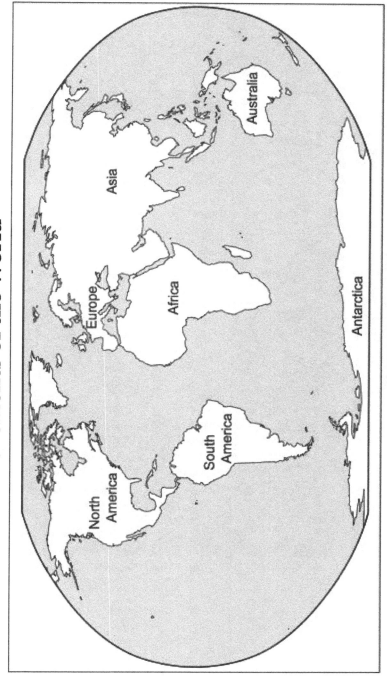

1977 – 2012: Kevin has hitchhiked around the world 9 times through 132 countries on all 7 continents.

Kevin has hitchhiked through all of the Americas.

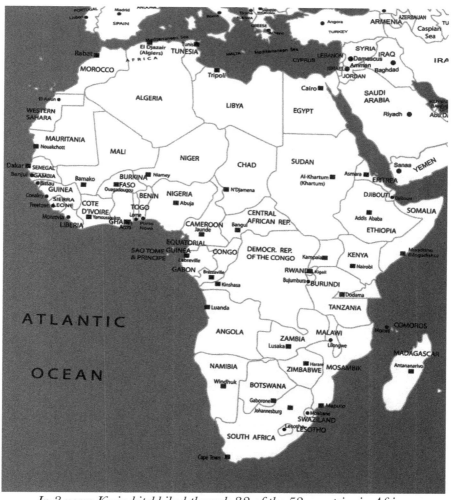

In 3 years Kevin hitchhiked through 32 of the 52 countries in Africa.

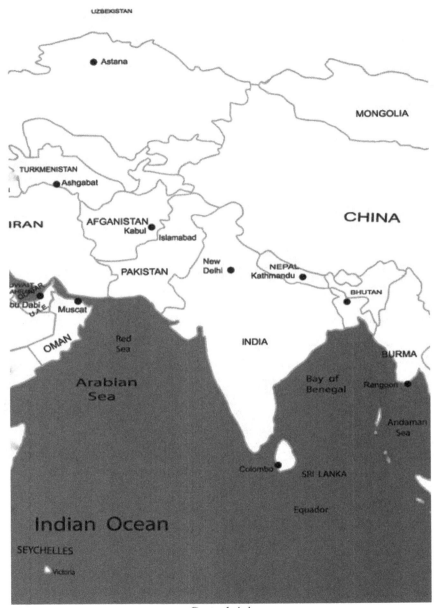

Central Asia

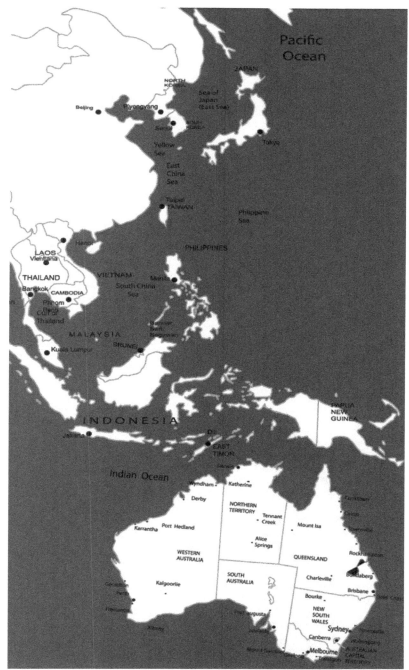

Southeast Asia & Australia

Table of Contents

Introduction

In 1969, the "Summer of Love" and the first man on the moon, I was nine years old, and all about my bike. The music and the movies promoted movement, freedom and wind in your hair. Inspired by the "Easy Rider" poster in my brother's bedroom, my chopper bike was a hodge-podge of recycled bicycles found at our local dump. The only things new on my bike were the banana seat and sissy bar, paid for with the proceeds from snow shoveling and selling retrieved golf balls at the local club.

It was on my way to find golf balls that I met my first freedom camping hitchhikers. Early one Saturday a couple was packing up from camping on the ninth hole. They crossed the street and I watched this beautiful girl with flowers in her hair and her boyfriend stick out their thumbs and confidently ask for a ride. Who knows, maybe they were headed just down the road to Woodstock. A year later I hitched for the first time with my cousin John. I was amazed at how easy it was to catch a ride the 5 miles into town, a whole lot easier than riding my "chopper."

In farm country in the '70s hitching was relatively safe and about the only way to get around. The summer after I turned 14, I hitched three hours to see the Old Man of the Mountain rock formation in New Hampshire. I had told my mom that I was going camping with a friend, but he bailed at the last minute so I went alone. Just north of Conway some small-town police detained me. They thought I was a teenage runaway and called my parents. A few weeks later my mom gave me written permission to hitch and my dad had it notarized. They knew I was going to do things on my own. The cage door had been opened and I was ready to fly.

When I was 16 years old, a friend of mine was going to the White Mountain School, an amazing bohemian boarding school that taught kayaking, ice climbing, rock climbing and skiing. I really wanted to attend and asked my parents if they would go halves with me on the tuition. I am the fifth of seven kids and my parents cringed at the thought of this expense. Later I found out my mom convinced my dad to send me because she thought that I didn't have the ability to go to college. With dyslexia, I wasn't exactly the sharpest tool in the shed, but I had a hell of a personality. I found it easy to meet people and seemed to fit into any crowd. That summer I joined my sister Karen in Bar Harbor, Maine and got a job clearing tables in a fancy restaurant in prestigious Acadia National Park. I would clear the tables, put any leftover food in my daypack and eat it later in order to save the $3,000, my promised half of the boarding school tuition. I remember one sunset down on the pier trying to get around the coleslaw to the half-eaten cheeseburger at the bottom of my doggy bag. Poverty never felt so good.

The last two weeks of my summer holiday I rewarded myself by taking a trip with one of Karen's adventuresome friends. We hitched 800 miles through the eastern provinces of Canada. I was thunderstruck. How easy it was to obtain rides with a beautiful 20-year-old girl! Who knew this would mark the next 35 years of my thumb in the air on all seven continents.

hitchhike | ˈhi ch ˌhīk|

verb [intrans.]
travel by getting free rides in passing vehicles:
he dropped out in 1976 and hitchhiked west.
noun
a journey made by hitchhiking.
DERIVATIVES
hitchhiker noun

My 52ⁿᵈ birthday 2012, Nepal

This collection of adventures is not in chronological order.
Enjoy the read.

-Kevin

1
African Spear Collection

As heard on National Public Radio's "The World"

In southern Ethiopia I visited a fly-infested market town. This weekly market attracts the most untamed tribe of Africa, the Hamar. The Hamar people are big, strong, black as cobalt blue and often naked. They look every bit the fearsome warriors they are reputed to be. Most of this tribe relies on bartering and very few have money. I was watching the afternoon unfold at the market and drinking a young corn beer out of a dried gourd cup, when a big naked Hamar warrior came right up to me and aggressively demanded that I buy him a beer. He was 6-foot three inches tall, with rippling muscles and car tire sandals. I stood up to change my view and replied jokingly with help from the beer-selling translator that I would buy him all the beer he wanted if he would give me his spear. To my amazement he agreed and that afternoon so did six of his buddies. By sunset, my fellow comrades and I had drunk a rusty bathtub worth of new corn beer and I had an authentic Ethiopian Hamar spear collection. At first the warrior's friends were offended and aggressive when I snapped their wooden shafts to slide their metal spearheads into my pack. But after the fourth or fifth time they began to cheer and dance with great excitement. To this day, I proudly display that drunken spear collection.

2
The Wandering Ambassador

You know how some simple encounters can change your life? I had one such experience in the late '80s when I was fortunate enough to paint the interior of a retired pilot's home in Florida. He received eight free airline tickets a year as part of his pension and was eager to turn them into cash. These "buddy passes" allow anyone to fly standby anywhere the airline travels. The deal he was offering me for painting was six buddy passes the first year and six more passes the following year at $50 each, which would be deducted from my bill. The downside with buddy passes is the unpredictable scheduling of traveling "stand-by." Additionally, being more of an overland traveler, I didn't fly that frequently. Still, I was interested. This old horse-trader was worthy of a good bartering partner, so I put on my best poker face and countered with, " I don't like to sleep in airports just to save a little money. How about two of your buddy passes per year, at $20 each, for the next 15 years? " He came back with 10 years at the same price and we shook on 12 years at $20 per buddy pass. Oh my god, I've died and gone to heaven! I wrote the deal in paint on the wall of his garage so he wouldn't forget. Two buddy passes a year for 12 years! I would've happily painted his entire house inside and out instead of the mere three rooms to which we had agreed. He thought I would be flying in the States, not the world. Rubbing salt into his wounds, he was flabbergasted when I sent him postcards from Asia, Australia and Africa over the next 12 years. We became good friends.

The reason this encounter was so significant for me as a traveler is because I quickly learned how to maximize these open-ended tickets at an astronomically low price. It was the major reason I could now travel eight months a year and work less to finance it. Not only that, I became adept at linking up destinations via the skyways. I was now a hitchhiker of the sky. I also discovered that camping in an airport really wasn't the nuisance I had anticipated. I like the energy at airports and I usually get bumped up to first class since economy is always the first to fill up. I go from my peanut butter and jelly sandwiches while waiting for an available seat to champagne and caviar while flying first class. I so appreciate the crazy contrasts life offers.

On my third time around the world, at 30,000 feet, with a heady little buzz, I congratulated myself on being an explorer and a wandering ambassador. Now having the luxury of going from one airport to another, I got off a plane in Seville, Spain and hitched down to Morocco. I was working my way back up to Madrid where I would fly on to Asia. I was picked up by a teacher, a young boy and a nun, who were traveling together in central Spain. The teacher was a 30-year-old Spanish man who spoke English well, liked to talk and was an intellectual. The young nun, who didn't understand English, pouted quietly and kept her eyes on the arid, rolling hills throughout the five-hour trip. The young boy in the backseat didn't know English either, but at five years old it wasn't a barrier and he and I played swords with straws.

There was a scarlet sunset streaking the horizon when they dropped me off in a working class suburb just south of Madrid. With the sun descending quickly, this was my last ride for the day. Tomorrow I would splurge for a bus, check out the city and then sleep at the airport. I was excited that the next leg of this adventure was in Asia. I studied the lay of the land to find the best approach for city camping. I crossed a busy street and headed into a vacant field in the middle of a neighborhood. I sat down in the tall grass and read my book in the day's remaining light, while waiting for nightfall to set up camp. But as night approached, the traffic worsened and pedestrians started cutting through the field. This was only the beginning of Friday night action and my intuition told me to move.

The feeling became overwhelming when two women began burning their household garbage near me.

With the obscurity of darkness as a cover, I walked along the dim shadows with biting mosquitoes plaguing me the entire way. Searching out a more suitable location, I hadn't gone far when I decided to set up my tent among a few thin trees. As usual, I put my money belt in a small, used plastic bag and stashed it twenty feet from my tent and quickly jumped inside for respite from the insects. Dogs were barking at a nearby house. The owner opened the gate and followed his dogs to my tent. I explained in Spanish that I was camping for one night only and flying out the next day. With a huff he grabbed up his dogs and dragged them back inside the yard. Now I was feeling uneasy about this spot, too!

Around 10 p.m. I heard the roar of a crowd and the crow of roosters and figured there was a cockfight somewhere nearby. After listening to this for a while, curiosity got the better of me. I crossed the street and got a drink and went to check out this crazy sport. I approached the circus tent from where all the commotion was coming. I could hear the boisterous shouts coming from the crowd. The ticket checker said something in Spanish. I pretended not to understand him and melted into the crowd. There was stifling heat and a cloudy haze of cigarette smoke inside the tent. The spectators were gathered around a small circular ring that was the center stage for this vicious 'sport.' Tension was at a feverish pitch as a lot of money was exchanging hands. Two men in the corner were attending a hooded rooster. One was keeping the competitor calm by constantly stroking its back and the other was lacing up a three-inch metal spur on the rooster's leg. I was watching the brutal exchange between a beautiful teal-colored bird clashing against a brilliant red one when the bouncer tapped me on the shoulder and told me I needed a ticket. I stalled him long enough to see the bloody outcome, then beat a hasty retreat.

In the welcoming fresh cool air outside the tent, I glanced up and noticed two hoodlums, bare-chested and drinking from a paper sack. They were eyeing me as I passed them. I was weary of the attention and headed back to the refuge of the field. I deliberately took an off-the-beaten path direction to avoid being followed. When I passed the tall grass I dropped and crawled for a while, but because of broken glass and garbage, I ended up having to stand up and walk the last thirty feet.

My intuition was still screaming at me. It had been a very bad idea to set up camp here and even worse to stray from it! Minutes after I'd gone into my tent I could hear footsteps. Someone began whacking the sides of my tent with a stick claiming to be the police. My heart pounded so quickly in my chest that I thought it might pop out of my mouth! I knew this wasn't the police, but the hoodlums from outside the cockfighting tent.

The dogs on the neighboring lot started going crazy again. One of the boys opened my tent and started punching me in the head. As I was trying to ward off his blows, the back entrance to my tent opened and his partner in crime began hitting me with a stick. They got me to my feet, patted me down, took my backpack, which held some clothes, camera and down jacket, and mugger money and ran off laughing. Mugger money refers to a small amount of cash I always keep accessible for the sole purpose of being robbed. These robbers might have lost all their money gambling at the cockfight but they easily recouped their losses at my expense. They had split my lip and broken my nose but I knew that my money belt was safe. Though somewhat shell-shocked, I was happy as hell that I didn't have any broken teeth, broken bones or need stitches. They hadn't gotten my money belt, which held my passport, traveler's checks, a wad of cash and my airline ticket. This battered ambassador would still fly to Asia tomorrow night.

3
Welcome to India

My taste for international travel came after attending the somewhat bohemian White Mountain School in New Hampshire. I was 16 and in awe of the rugged landscape and the international students. It was at the boarding school that I was also introduced to rock climbing. After graduating in 1979, my best friend Rob and I decided to bike through Europe.

Rob and I began in England. Keeping to the back roads through tiny rural villages, we cycled from London to Barcelona, Spain. By the time we crossed over into Switzerland, the bicycle had become an encumbrance because of the huge Alps. Rob and I found friendly farmers who let us stash our bikes so we could hitch around for a few days and return to reclaim them later.

The Italians love their bicycles and hitchhiking in bike gear helped tremendously. We meandered through the hills of Tuscany, flirting with Italy's wine and women. We felt like men of the world. We slept mainly in our tent and occasionally in stone barns.

After months of travel we flew to Seattle. It was late autumn and I stayed with Rob's loving family and we found work laying asphalt. It was rough and dirty work and by winter Rob and I traded tar for snow as cross-country ski instructors in White Pass, Washington. Rob was my boss and he coached all the good skiers and the pretty girls while I taught their parents. On our many days off we skied the backcountry, cutting trails through the thigh-high snow that covered incredibly steep slopes. The vastness of this backcountry wilderness was mind blowing.

The following year I left the west coast to attend college in an uninspiring New England mill town. Studying business in the cold rain depressed me. College was just okay. My true passion was travel. How I longed for the open road. For four years I jumped around from the east coast to the west coast and back to the east, studying everything from business to civil engineering to art and architecture. I finally came to the realization that I needed to trade in my books for a passport and a backpack. Enough is enough. Kevin, follow your heart. I loved to paint big houses for appreciative people for too much money and travel the world. That's my heart song. And so it started. In the summers I always make great money with my own painting business, which continues today. I discovered that six months of work could finance six months of travel and I later refined this to four months of work and eight months of travel. I had money in my pocket and the world was mine. Life was grand!

My earliest half-year adventure was to Central America in 1984. I teamed up with my buddy Mark, a motorcycle racer and mechanic. He repaired an old, broken-down van, which we named the "Dodge Lodge" that took us deep into Central America. We soon discovered some significant problems with this mode of transport. It involved entirely too much driving and isolated us from the very people we wanted to meet. Day after day we spent looking out the same bug-encrusted, dusty windshield, listening to the same cassette tape over and over—Bob Seger's "Kathmandu." The stress of protecting the van and paying for fuel took away from our adventure.

On our way back home, the Dodge Lodge left us stranded on the side of a road in the mountains of Central Mexico. Loading up our essential gear in backpacks, Mark and I abandoned the van and everything else we had accumulated in this rolling can. We split what was left of our money, said good-bye to each other and solo hitched the 4,000 miles from Acapulco back to Boston.

What a difference hitching made! The adventure truly doubled in size from this point forward. I was no longer imprisoned by the van and I started to hang out with the locals whom I had longed to meet. I learned how humbling it is to be dependent on the good will of poor people and this simple fact helped shape my approach to travel for the next 30 years. It gave me ever-increasing courage to broaden my horizons.

In 1985 I took on Asia, again with Mark, and it did not involve a bike or a van: just a backpack, a thumb and a smile! When we landed in the Bombay airport I was immediately overwhelmed by so many new sensations: smells, colors, oppressive heat, dilapidated buses jammed with people and rickshaw drivers grabbing for business. Only the tourists were wearing Western dress. India was far more exotic than I had ever dreamed possible. My momentary trepidation turned into fascination.

Twenty minutes into riding the roof of the airport bus into the city, I saw my first plastic slum. It was a scavenger's collection of sticks, bricks, plastic and tin. In the blackened doorway of one home was a truly beautiful woman dressed in a red sari, adorned with massive quantities of gold in her nose and ears. She looked like a princess in an unlikely setting. I learned that she was wearing her wedding dowry to keep it safe in her slum neighborhood where doors don't have locks.

At the very end of the slum, close to the road, was an old man dressed in brilliant white bed sheet-like traditional Churidar clothing. He had a massive handlebar mustache, perfectly waxed at both ends and wore a rainbow-colored turban with huge gold earrings. In all his elegant glory, he was squatting for his morning dump! A young boy, dressed exactly the same, was squatting next to him. The old man looked up at the bus, saw us on the roof and with a big wave and an even bigger smile shouted, "Welllcomme to Innndia!"

It was in India that I came to the realization that there is far more to experience if I step outside of my comfort zone. For all the seeming horrors of the slums, outdoor shitters, dead animals and corrupt police, I also witnessed the incredible diversity of India's tolerant people. The varying regions of India differ in costume, religion and culture, but throughout, their open curiosity and friendliness towards outsiders makes for the most interesting population I have ever encountered. It was wonderfully intoxicating.

Adding to the tremendous contrasts of this subcontinent are the extreme differences in climate, landscape and architecture, from the snowy Himalayas to the blistering desert to the humidity of Kerala's waterways. The vast array of architecture is representative of the major religions. With access to easily carved sandstone, artisans and stonemasons have been creating temples, art and shrines for thousands of years. Halfway around the world I was feeling giddy and tranquil at the same time. I was completely in awe of India's spirituality. It touched my soul.

Eight months later, having hitched the USA, England, France, Germany, Holland, India, Bangladesh, Thailand, China and back across the United States, I had completed my first trip around the world! I was 25 years old and completely and utterly addicted to international travel. India had changed me forever. No longer did I view the world through ethnocentric eyes. I was caught up in a fresh rhythm of life and realized that the world is full of wonder.

"Not all those who wander are lost." -Tolkien

Jain religion, India

4

West African Brothels

In 2002 I flew into West Africa, which sees few travelers, for another eight-month trip. Since I do little research, it wasn't a complete surprise to find upon arrival that Cote d'Ivoire was in a state of civil unrest and about to undergo a political coup. The four days I spent in this metropolis truly blew my mind. People from all over the continent worked in this famed "New York City of Africa." It was a magical mix of business suits and traditional clothing, African and jazz music and outdoor cafes. My favorite French café featured amazing people-watching. All the waiters wore their country's colorful wrap, and their smiling faces were adorned by tribal scarring. My French was bad and it took me a few days to realize everyone seemed to be talking nervously about the upcoming coup. That's when I decided it was time to get out of Cote d'Ivoire. From Ghana, I slowly traveled through the tiny countries of Togo and Benin. From there, I headed inland to Burkina Faso.

I was getting around mostly by hitching the 6-and 10-wheel cargo trucks that carry everything from flour to concrete. These trucks were slow and old with cracked windshields and worn tires. The trick was not to get in the cab but to ride the toolbox above the driver in order to have the most spectacular view of the passing scenery. I could be charged too much to ride these giant lumbering dinosaurs or nothing at all. Often there were local men on board as they moved around to find work or to return to their homes.

At that time, French West Africa had a food shortage and restaurants were scarce. I primarily ate small translucent chicken eggs, which I bought from street vendors who sold them fried on white bread. Often I would buy a few dozen and pay extra to have them boiled up. It seemed I lived on nothing but eggs, 10 or 12 boiled eggs a day for over half a year; a fried-egg sandwich was a luxury. I called them protein pellets.

In the countryside I slept in my tent, but in the cities I needed safety from the streets and found the only rooms I could regularly afford were in the brothels. One of my favorite brothels in West Africa was in a small city in the country of Burkina Faso, which seems as far from any civilized portion of the earth as one can get! Traversing barren lands that held little water, it was an old town rising out of the open plains. "La Moustache" is a tired, classic colonial saloon with a bar downstairs and rooms for rent upstairs, and at sunset on a Friday night it was the rockin'est place in town. Knowing but 50 words of the French language I was in a state of hyper-awareness, constantly relying on my intuition. Perched in the far corner of the main saloon with my back to the wall pretending to read a book, I was trying to be an inconspicuous spectator. This tiny bar was loud and lively, filled with dark-skinned rascals draining their week's wages.

Then it happened. Claudette approached me. At 6'2", well over 200 pounds, with purple mascara and breasts like torpedoes, she was an exclamation that defied translation. This imposing giant of a woman had her hair wrapped in large, fluorescent curlers of various colors and was considered a true beauty queen in this part of Africa. Knowing that here was a place with a 20 percent AIDS rate, she was not exactly what this skinny white guy was looking for. The cold shoulder treatment had no effect on Claudette and she inched closer. With her bold attitude and even bolder cleavage at eye level, I was looking for a diversion to diplomatically excuse myself from her company. My escape came as the chambermaid, a beautiful African Cinderella, was just finishing cleaning up a room. I grabbed my pack, said my good-byes, darted around Claudette, paid the bartender for the room and scurried up the stairs past Cinderella.

One can either take a room by the hour or for the night. You are either in or out, as there are no room keys. In this tiny grubby room I set up my tent on the bed. I wondered about the variety of acts that had been enjoyed on this very tired mattress. I opened the door and yelled downstairs to the bartender to get his attention and ordered a beer. Cinderella brought it up to me and cast an astonished glance at the tent erected on the bed. Later, I ordered a second Guinness. When I opened the door for Cinderella it was my turn to stare. Accompanying her were six or more wide-eyed, astonished working girls. They were peering through the slightly opened door, their heads stacked totem pole-style, one on top of the other, finishing with Claudette's fluorescent curlers. They were staring in disbelief at the tent on the bed and looked at me as if I had parked a spaceship in their courtyard.

Practicing her one English word, Claudette batted her purple eyelashes and said, "Free, monsieur, free." Smiling, I softly closed the door, finished my beer and slept like a baby. At the crack of dawn, with the sound of street sweepers as my alarm clock, I quietly left and found my rhythm in the reassuring arms of a new day.

Muhammad: "With five children we come here to be intimate."

5
Big-Wall Hardman

1997 found me in Yosemite Valley, California where I stayed at the climber's camp for a week. This valley is one of the prettiest places I have ever been: animals, wildflowers and huge waterfalls are surrounded by the grandeur of rock faces. At 37 years old, I was at the height of my climbing career. I was enjoying the international company around a fire in the middle of August. Some Swiss climbers had just summited El Capitan and the food and the wine were flowing. A tall, red-bearded Scotsman pulled up a chair and started talking. His name was Stuart and a few days earlier he had summited El Capitan with his Italian partner. He said that they were planning on doing the Direct North Buttress in the early morning, but from the look of things his partner was sidetracked with an American girl and a jug of wine.

Later in the evening, to my amazement, Stuart asked me if I was up for the climb. I turned to face this gentle giant as I was digesting his offer. He expanded on the features of the route, "Two thousand feet of face and chimney climbing with roughly twenty 5.10 rated pitches. We'll be off tomorrow night, God willing." The way he said 'God willing' in his thick Scottish brogue gave me the slightest tinge of apprehension. I responded, "While I'm by no means a Yosemite Crack Master, if you're up for leading it, I think I can second it." We walked to my tent to evaluate my rack. The only gear of mine that Stuart was interested in were my five big cams. We said goodnight and agreed to meet at 4:30 the following morning, which was only six hours away. The willy-nillys of what I had just signed up for made for a very restless night's sleep.

As promised, Stuart showed up with all his gear and headlamp on and we drove out to the approach of the DNB (Direct North Buttress), barely discernible for the lack of stars peering into the valley. I was trying to be jovial, despite the lack of sleep, not to mention the twenty pounds of water and Snickers bars weighing me down. I so needed a cup of coffee, but adrenaline would have to do. We made our way to the base at 5:30 as the few stars sputtered out, fading into dawn.

Our initial plan was to swing lead, which meant that we alternated leading each pitch. I thought that would be manageable even though I knew 5.11 was my maximum ability. Stuart would start us out because he knew the particular difficulty of the third pitch. The first pitch went well so we traded off the rack and the pack. Still needing my headlamp to guide me in the dim light, I meticulously placed protection frequently and carefully. Stuart whizzed up right behind me and in his resonant Scottish accent called to my attention what a glorious day it was starting out to be. He commented on what a wonderful job I did leading and announced firmly, yet politely, that he would be leading the rest of the pitches. Had I been inclined to argue, the wisdom of his suggestion would have become all too apparent on the next pitch.

The start of the third pitch, the famous *Supertopo,* involved a dynamic move off a greasy handhold straight off the belay. Before Stuart could set his first piece of protection, he was confronted by an off-balance under-cling leading straight to a semi-blind smooth sloper. He had to pitch his body horizontally to negotiate the difficulty of this section. If Stuart were to fall here, he would be severely injured. This crux was the most dangerous part of the climb! Listening to the grunts and groans of my lead man, I half expected Stuart to come down on top of me. With 2,000 feet and 20 pitches left to go, the magnitude of this undertaking was setting in. Even in the predawn hours, I knew we would be using every bit of daylight!

The biggest challenge of the DNB is deciphering the direction of the climbing route. While the route description itself is adequate, it tells you nothing of the huge features nearby to help with orientation. The third pitch was a bitter breakfast, and we decided to make the top of the ninth pitch our lunchtime goal. The lower section of this climb was way more sustained crack climbing than I expected and consistently in the 5.10 range. Adding to the level of danger were a few sections of the climb where our only option was to use very old, rusty fixed gear.

Well into the sixth pitch, hundreds of feet off the deck, I looked between my legs and saw a team of climbers below, coming up fast. Finishing the pitch sweaty and tired, I met up with Stuart at the anchor. We both watched in awe as this team was overcoming us using a simultaneous climbing technique. I had only read about this and had never witnessed it. They were literally climbing three times as fast as we were. This technique of climbing means that each climber ascends at the same pace with a hundred feet of rope between them. Placing minimal protection, these skilled hard men were impressive to observe. Stuart joked that they would surely be sleeping in their own beds tonight. At the top of the eighth pitch at 2:00 pm, the bronzed, big-wall cowboys passed us with a wink and a nod. Stuart and I just looked at each other. Being first on the route is key for both mental comfort and avoiding falling rocks. Now that they were above us, we had to worry about them dropping loose rock on us. I passed Stuart a Snickers bar and the jug of water and we both started laughing. It was a welcome release of tension.

Climbing as fast as we could, we reached the top of the ninth pitch around 3:00 p.m. Although we still had several hours of light, we knew that at our present pace the likelihood of spending the night on the cliff was significant. Even though I was climbing very slowly, I was nurtured by my partner's optimism and confidence. I was in the middle of a serious adventure in one of the most beautiful climbing spots in the world. There were a thousand vertical feet below me and a thousand vertical feet above! The exposure and quality of climbing was perfect, and the twelfth pitch was exceptional. I could hear the voices of the climbers on El Cap echoing off the granite. I truly felt like a 'Big Waller.'

We were finished with the thousand feet of face climbing and were now looking to go into the rock - a huge crack system of vertical caves. It got weird and very strenuous. On DNB the true wrestling is only beginning on the face and we had some trouble determining where to traverse into the chimney slot. I have a serious allergy to vertical rock shafts and they were on me like a bad rash, but once I adopted the right attitude they were well worth the effort. In these tight quarters, I had no choice but to trail the now lighter pack 3 feet beneath me. The upper chimneys are physically demanding and should've gone fairly quickly, but as the day wore on I was running out of steam.

On the sixteenth pitch, back out on the exposed vertical face, we finished the last of our food and water while watching the sun quickly disappear from the valley. With the last of the light, Stuart scouted out a place to sleep. Without overnight gear, we laid down our ropes and Stuart banged a piton in for an extra anchor. He then cleverly attempted to web us in a sitting position on a tiny, 2 foot sloping ledge with slings and ropes. Our bodies were pitched forward in the makeshift safety net and we were dangling over 1,700 vertical feet above the valley floor. It was more than a little difficult to relax! Thankfully August provides long days and warm nights in the valley. We watched the traffic below and talked about our climb's highpoints until, slumped over, we gave in to exhaustion.

The following morning I awoke with very stiff muscles and a bit of a headache from dehydration and day two of no caffeine, but I was eager to finish. Stuart, the rugged Scot, was in his element. By the time he was racked we both had a strong case of summit fever. In comparison to yesterday's 16 pitches, today's last six rated 5.6 to 5.7, which should have been quite manageable. However, without nourishment this easy upper section seemed the same as yesterday to me: sustained and exhausting. By high noon we finally made it to the top and screamed a victory cry that echoed off the massive wall a mile away.

Stuart and I knew that the descent is when rock climbers most often get killed. The trick to getting off the mountain is route-finding because the scale of the rock formation is so grand it's hard to get any perspective. Our exhaustion led to bad judgment and being off-route, which led to lots of loose rock. After four long hours we finally made it off the cliff and onto the proper hiking trail. We were beyond ecstatic! On wobbly legs it took us another two hours to walk several more miles to my car.

Tradition holds that successful 'Big Wallers' conclude their climb at the All-You-Can-Eat Buffet on the edge of town. Climbers think nothing of entering this eatery right after a climb in their smelly attire and dirt-encrusted, taped fingers. Even though every ounce of my strength was sapped, gorging on mountains of meat and buckets of beer sounded like a great idea. I was on my heaping second plate when the Italians came bursting through the door, boisterous and jubilant from their triumph on El Cap. It took the Italians four days to summit the famous El Capitan. They knew Stuart and began good-naturedly harassing him about getting stuck on DNB. He responded that it had been our original intention to maximize the pleasure. With the back-slappin' camaraderie of a bunch of bandits, the raucous Italians were having none of it and accused us of not being able to find the catwalk, which we wildly denied. In between large mouthfuls of food and generous swills of beer, the rowdy discussion continued with a group of Canadians just in to join the celebration. I was basking in the infamy of Big Wall jargon with these seasoned Vikings at the victory feast. However, when one such renegade turned his attention to me and asked pointedly if El Cap was my next pursuit, I choked and tried to conceal the flush creeping up my neck. Controlling the high-pitch squeak my voice had taken on, I croaked out, "Maybe…" He didn't know I was an imposter, and I wasn't ready to admit it because tonight I was a 'Big-Wall Hardman' in the present company!

Climbing in Yosemite

6
Mauritania

———

In 1659 St. Louis was the first French settlement in West Africa. Even today this colonial town is the last northern frontier in Senegal. Narrow cobblestone streets outline the two-story stone homes with huge wooden doors dressed up in elaborate rod iron designs and capped off with roofs of terra cotta tiles. Very little traffic was going north in 2002, and after waiting a full week for a ride, I was feeling very anxious. Waiting that long for a ride is like being caught in the doldrums on a sailboat hoping for a breeze: it's hard on the spirit. I ended up paying a young taxi driver to help me find a ride for my journey through the country of Mauritania into Morocco, possibly a two-week trip.

Very early the next morning I was awakened by Pierre the taximan. "Come quick, the best one so far," he said in French. I quickly packed, paid my bill and we sped off together. At a bed-and-breakfast on the other side of town were two young men loading the roof of a white Land Rover. The gasoline cans and the desert jack told me they were going the distance through the most remote northern country of Africa: Mauritania. Among travelers, Mauritania is legendary for its Orthodox Muslims, extreme deserts and the barren, sandy tracks that pass for roads. With a wink to Pierre and a short prayer composed in my heart I walked over to this pair as the morning light was breaking. "Bonjour, are you boys going north?" I asked. They looked me over and one of them grunted, "yes." I tried again and said, "I'm a rich American looking for a ride to Morocco on the roof of your car." The taller one started laughing. "That's good, mate, because we don't have any room inside, do we,

Thomas?" Thomas didn't even look up from his work. I had one more chance to snag this ride or endure another long, lonely wait. "I've got gas money for this expedition. I'm an excellent photographer, a terrible cook, and a great pot washer. I'm an overlander trying to link up Africa and I really need this ride on your roof." I gave them my best puppy dog eyes. The tall man then asked, "Is it legal to ride the roof in Mauritania?" I didn't know if he was kidding and replied that I'd been doing it for the past year coming up from South Africa. When Thomas finally spoke in his heavy French accent, he said, "Give us a little space so we can talk about it." I walked back to the taxi. Five long minutes later they came over and we discussed a few more details and with no apparent conflicts, I had my ride. I found out the taller one's name was Stephan, and he was much more sociable and easier to understand than Thomas.

My companions on the roof of the Land Rover were two gas cans, a spare tire and a large metal tool box. I tied my pack down to the sturdy frame of the luggage rack and rode it like a saddle. With my hat and sunglasses firmly in place, I was ready to go. Crossing the border from Senegal into Mauritania was no problem, but in the short distance it took to reach Rosso, the southernmost city of Mauritania, we encountered numerous checkpoints. While the police had no problem with me riding the roof, we were continually asked for the vehicle's papers, passports and conversation but no bribe money. Truly un-African!

North of Rosso we veered inland and after an hour or so, roadblocks were no longer an issue. In fact, civilization ended. For a decade now, little rain had fallen and the earth was sunbaked dry. Along the single-track that passed for a road there were no people, no bushes, no animals, no water, no nothing. Mile after mile we drove, on the outermost edge of the Sahara. If we broke down we would be dead a few days after our water ran out. The three of us young guys were heading into unexpected lands without any concept of what we would find, but we all knew it would be an adventure we could handle.

After long hours of slow driving, the sun turned the dunes to an amazing warm orange and we pulled a couple feet off the track to set up our evening camp. We didn't have the luxury of a fire since there wasn't any wood to be found, but the provisions we did have included a small gas stove. Thomas had a surplus of spices and turned out to be a wonderful cook. We erected our tiny tents under the expanse of an infinite sky and with full bellies slept soundly.

As the vapors on the horizon took shape the next morning, I made out the unmistakable form of distant camels. Stephan ran for the binoculars and when we focused the quarter of a mile separating us from the caravan, we could clearly see the desert people toiling for their living. Salt mines are among the few resources this region possesses, and two men wearing heavy woolen jallabiyas were transporting the precious commodity across the desert. Each man was riding a camel, and the other 20 camels were carrying four-foot round salt slabs tethered to their sides. Crossing the desert on a camel seems so archaic. However, knowing sand is a machine's worst enemy, I would put money on the camel for reliability. Our machine was holding up admirably through the tortuous terrain, nonetheless I silently sent up a little prayer for our mode of transportation.

With great dunes to the east and the mighty Atlantic to the west, we continued. A couple of days and a couple of hundred miles into our adventure Stephan began joining me up on the roof through the endless stretches of desert; in return he offered me his passenger seat, which was a welcome respite from the sun and wind. Thomas had also loosened up and to my surprise on the fifth evening let me drive as he joined Stephan on the roof. It was Thomas's first time on the roof and my first time at the wheel and by watching their shadows I could tell we were all having the time of our lives.

The Land Rover was slow but powerful in four-wheel drive as we slid up and over the miles of hypnotic dunes. I was driving in the middle of nowhere on a road navigating by GPS. Then we came upon an incredible sight. In the distance, glowing in the golden light of sunset was a tiny oasis marked by the shadows of surrounding date palms. Parked under the trees was a beat-up sandblasted 10-wheel cargo truck packed to the gills with goods. I rolled up quietly and turned off the engine. A dozen Muslim men were getting ready to pray. Muhammad says in the Koran that you must wash before praying, but if there's no water or temple, good Muslims will wash their hands and feet in sand before praying toward Mecca. From our perch on top of the Land Rover we watched their quiet moments of worship.

Later the Muslims invited us to camp with them. We cooked, ate and talked around the campfire. I found out through the interpretations of Stephan that the assembly of men gathered there were representative of all four of Mauritania's castes. The top caste was the tan Arab driver; then the black Africans; then the emancipated slaves; and finally, the slaves still in ownership. In 1980 Mauritania was the last place on earth to ban slavery and yet there's an estimated 100,000 slaves still in service in this archaic country. At my urging, Stephan talked to the truck boy who was dressed in rags and confirmed that he really was the property of the Arab driver. In the expanse of the desert night my wondering heart could not reconcile the concept of human ownership; it fell as short as a rock thrown to the stars.

The next day the landscape changed to loose sand on rocky, barren plateaus punctuated with random oases. The landscape was no longer void of trees. Bushes and birds and a small adobe village announced our return to civilization. I noticed a few green gardens bordering the occasional whitewashed house with wells and fairly clean children. The more water, the cleaner the kids, and it was great to be around both again.

We needed to stop here to replenish our supplies. Spotting a big well in the front yard of one of the homes, Thomas began bartering with the woman of the house. I showed her our four five-gallon water jugs and we balked at the price she quoted to refill them. The Muslim woman, though shy, remained firm, and finally we understood that the price of the muddy water included her labor. Using a bucket and rope attached to the deep well to retrieve twenty gallons of water was a huge task that would take the better part of an hour. We agreed to the woman's offer, then drove down the road to find diesel.

The gas station was nothing more than a thatched structure filled with greasy 55-gallon drums. The owner used a hand crank to extract the liquid from the drums into one-gallon mason jars. A rag and a funnel were lying in the corner, and a sweaty little Arab kid who could be called our attendant put the rag in the big metal funnel and gently poured the diesel from the mason jar into our tank. It took 30 jars to fill up the tank and reserve cans. We split the cost three ways and hoped the quality of the fuel was better than it looked. In the time it took to replenish the diesel supply, our water woman was ready for us and threw in dates and a wave as we headed off. The sight of a sleeping boy in the branches of a dead tree was another stark image etched in my mind as we left this two-camel town.

On the eighth day the topography changed once again as we lost the road that was now pinned against the beach. Every six hours we had to wait for the tide to go out to continue our journey. We traveled at this intermittent pace for two days. At one point we were driving on the hard-packed sand of the beach while I dozed on the roof. We came over a rise only to find a pond of saltwater on the other side. Thomas hit the brakes hard and slammed into the two-foot-deep pond, catapulting me over the hood and into the saltwater. Thank God I didn't break my ass on the roof rack and cleared the hood. I was so close to getting run over!

The next section of the rutted dirt road was harder to find. The only way we knew we were still on route, apart from our GPS, were a few broken-down cars and old tires being consumed by the sand. Once again we found ourselves traversing barren lands that held no water. This hundred-mile stretch of latitude was sparse and seemed hot enough to blister the paint off a moving vehicle.

We finally snaked inland, moving painfully slow over broken rocks and a gravel riverbed that was now the road. Neither of my traveling companions was inclined to give up the springs of their cushioned seats over this stretch, and the relentless, teeth-rattling ride was wearing on my sore and sunburned body. The direction straightened as we descended from yet another rise, and I noticed we were now parallel with a set of railroad tracks. I was so relieved that we were no longer tangled in the corkscrew turns of the dry riverbed. Squinting into the distance, I could make out the contours of a giant iron horse perched on her tracks. The impressive length of this train, which runs regularly from the iron mines of Zouerate to the coast of Nouadhibou, is 1.4 miles, the longest in the world. At this time the train was heading back empty to Zouerate and its only cargo was the characters riding the roof and hanging out of its doorways. I looked upon them with envy. This ragged bunch of desert dogs looked so carefree with their loose-fitting garments flapping in the wind. It seemed to me that I was a prisoner chained to the roof and to my two French companions.

By sunset the next day we had reached the famous town of Chinguetti. It was founded in 777 AD and is an historically significant caravan town in the Sahara. It is the seventh holiest city of Islam. Today, however, this UNESCO World Heritage-designated city of 4,700 inhabitants has no more salt, camels, scholars or gold. Like Timbuktu, the sands of time have erased this once intellectual hub of culture and commerce. Goat's milk and dates are some of the few pleasures Chinguetti now offers, along with its beautiful mosques and a few dozen minarets. The abundance of shade from the crumbling buildings stacked closely on narrow streets was a welcome relief from the constant sun. At sunset a local guide joined us at our campsite. He told us the Moors of northern Africa were at the height of their culture, wisdom and knowledge at the same time that Europe was seeing its collapse during the Dark Ages. These Muslims preserved and developed astronomy, math and medicine and later shared their advances with Europe. We enjoyed the history lesson on the edge of the dunes engulfing this forgotten city.

On our twelfth sun-scorched day of travel we reached the Moroccan border, which welcomed us with a seven-foot wide paved road! After seven months of stumbling through the foreign territories of Cote d'Ivoire, Ghana, Togo, Benin, Burkina Faso, Niger, Mali, Senegal and Mauritania with the most basic equipment, limited French and even less money, I was looking forward to leaving West Africa far behind. This was the hardest trip I had made to date and I had survived; a bit battered and sun-blistered, though not dispirited. I was ecstatic to have another month left to make Spain via the delights of Morocco.

At the Moroccan border two young customs agents, clearly desperate for company, welcomed us enthusiastically at a makeshift border patrol station. It seemed amazing that an international checkpoint was comprised of a canvas tent with two cots and a table on a sandy floor. The agents weren't Mauritanian but Moroccan college graduates and both were serving their two-year mandatory military service. They were from the famous sophisticated Marrakesh, one of the few thriving caravan cities left in Africa. They spoke fluent English, and we talked and partied with them late into the night. The 'paved' road from which we would embark the following morning would be a luxury. That night we sang Madonna's "Material Girl" at full volume with the hash-smoking customs agents, reassuring me that after 220 days, I was officially back in the 20th century.

Mauritania Camel Market

7
Smugglers

For over a year I had been traveling around the world through Asia, Europe, and then sailing from Africa to South America. Now I was trying to get up the Amacuro delta from Venezuela to Guyana and then on to Suriname. Suriname would be the last of the Americas for me! In the town of Curiapo, I found the captain of a 40-foot open sugar boat who promised me passage up the delta for $10 a day. The tired old boat looked pretty cool: a tiny diesel with no paint; it reminded me of Bogart and Hepburn's *African Queen*. The deal was that I would work a little and bring my own food. "We are leaving tomorrow and it's a five-day trip," the captain said. It seemed too good to be true and, as it turned out, it was. A day's wait turned out to be four, and the afternoon rains started to depress me. The waiting seemed endless in this steamy, tropical town. On the fourth day, we finally began the voyage.

The first day out the four crewmen tending the boat helped themselves to all my food, leaving us only sugar, tea, green plantains and six loaves of white bread for the rest of the journey. It also became apparent that the boat had a terrible leak and was slowly sinking. The captain put us to work in shifts, bailing the boat with a five-gallon bucket. We had to bail a few gallons every five minutes, day and night. It was exhausting.

The second day, amidst the immense old-growth jungle, I began seeing the indigenous delta tribes in small three-person dugout canoes. As we chugged by, the natives discreetly hid in the mangroves at the river's edge. These were the Warao Indians, a loincloth culture that inhabit northeastern Venezuela and western

Guyana. The term Warao translates as 'the boat people,' corresponding to the Warao's lifelong intimate connection with the water.

In their dugout canoes two Waraos paddle and the third passenger sitting in the middle of the canoe will often hold up a leafy tree branch as a sail, catching the passing breezes to move them up the river. The canoe is the Warao's only means of transportation. Other modes such as walking are hampered by the hundreds of streams, rivulets, marshes and high waters created by the delta. It is said Warao babies often learn to swim before they learn to walk!

The river was a labyrinth of archipelagos, but thankfully the captain knew where he was going. As we continued our journey it began to occur to me that this was an incredible amount of effort to get sugar from one place to another. Suspicious, I asked the captain questions and found out that beneath the sacks of sugar was a re-built diesel engine, which the captain intended to sell in Guyana. Finally, the captain confided that his final mission was to smuggle the engine to a broken-down logging truck located deep in the jungle to avoid payment of the 100 percent duty required for all merchandise passing into Guyana.

By the third day I was exhausted from bailing and my waterlogged hands were starting to peel. The afternoon heat and humidity were intense and the open boat offered no shade. Every evening we were viciously munched by mosquitoes. I was extremely sunburned, dehydrated, hungry and had severe gas from the green plantains. Thank God I liked my fellow crewmen and they liked me. Everyone pulled their own weight bailing, but we were in the middle of nowhere in a very leaky boat!

On the fourth day the leak dramatically worsened and the captain said we needed to unload the sugar at a thatched fishing shack on a bamboo dock. Overly suspicious of us, the Warao men, with bows drawn, came rushing out of the thatched house, while the women and children retreated into the jungle. The captain spoke up to assure them we were peaceful and after a while it seemed that a bargain was struck. We unloaded 2,000 pounds of sugar onto their rickety bamboo dock. The captain barely suppressed his anger when

I showed the children the sweetness of the white sugar. I imagine the captain was sure his entire cargo would disappear once the locals understood its value. Part of the money bargain the captain struck for storing his cargo included not only the Warao's smoked fish, but also fruits and vegetables from the wild orchards of the delta. After four days of subsisting on the diet we had rationed out, these treats were beyond delicious.

I pointed to an unusually large tree lying by the shore, which was in the process of being hollowed out. One Warao spoke a bit of Spanish and explained the arduous boat making procedure. Bongos, as these boats are called, are about 60 feet long and eight feet wide and can hold up to 50 people! When an old bongo is worn beyond use a consensus is reached by the male household leaders as to which new tree will be harvested to replace the retired bongo. The process begins by finding a massive old-growth tree on the river's edge. At the start of the dry season the perfect tree is found and killed by cutting the bark around its base. At the end of the dry season the tree is cut down. Then, the tree is hollowed out by charring the interior and carved out using stone tools from the mountains. He said they bartered the tools for river fish. I was fascinated by these primitive stone chisels, which looked as if they had been in use since the dawn of time.

Relieved of the sugar load, we went to our first tiny village and arranged to have the boat hauled out for repairs. I realized we were already in Guyana. Two customs officers appeared out of nowhere and discovered that half our crew had no papers and that our boat was loaded with an illegal engine! The boat was impounded and the captain and crew were taken to jail. Thankfully the captain explained to the authorities that I was just a passenger and was not involved in his illegal enterprise. I later learned that the two customs officers faked the paperwork for the captain and had him pay roughly one-tenth the price of the normal duty that it would have cost at the official border. Everybody was happy. The customs officers quickly made up a scam about me needing a river permit and demanded $100 from me. After an hour of intense negotiations I paid them only $40 and then was let go.

With no other choice, I pitched my tent next to the customs shack that doubled as the jail and hoped my luck would change. I purchased a live rooster, had it fried and washed it down with rusty cans of warm beer. This little border town was so remote it had no roads in or out and was accessible only by the river. I even saw a Warao family pay their grocery bill with gold dust. After only a few days, with much discussion and bartering, I found a boat ride out of the border village. I paid way too much for it, but my new ride was legal, fast, free of leaks and heading directly towards the small port town of Morawhanna on the main road. Smugglers, naked Indians, corrupt officials, and a very leaky boat - now *that* was a backwater trip!

A young Warao boy selling bananas

8
The Watering Hole

On my fourth month camping through southern Africa, a local rancher tipped me off about a remote watering hole on the savannah. It was a day's hike off the main road. Instead of walking to the watering hole, I decided to wait for Saturday, hoping to hitch a ride with a tour group. Sure enough, the weekend crowd showed up. I flagged down a Land Rover and talked the guide into a ride to the watering hole.

There was no room inside the vehicle or on the roof rack, so I rode the bumper and hung onto the luggage ladder. The problem with riding a bumper on the savannah is that it's hard to breathe, or even see, in the whirlwind of dust. The second problem is fatigue. At the time, I didn't know we had 15 miles to go. The potholes, the dust, and the passing brush all conspired to shake me from my precarious hold.

Eventually the road led to rolling grasslands that opened up before us. We came to a plateau, and my tired arms gratefully let go of the truck. The grassland gave way to a baked ring of mud that made up the diminishing waterhole. The guide explained that this was a very active viewing spot for animals. Because there had been little rain for the past 10 years, it was one of the few remaining watering holes in the region.

Looking down about 200 feet away we could see a few lazy hippos visible only by their twitching ears and nostrils in the murky water. Waiting in the heat of the day, a small herd of eland finally came down to drink. I was awed by the beauty of the graceful deer-like creatures. Then the incredibly majestic scene became tainted with the actions of a half-dozen frenzied photographers. Although there were several hours of sun left, the guide herded his reluctant tourists to the Land Rover and back to the capital city without me. This was way too awesome to leave.

Equipped with nothing more than my tent, headlamp, Swiss army knife, water, some smelly goat cheese and a big bag of kudu jerky, I had mixed emotions standing alone, watching the taillights fade away. My first thought was that I finally had this secluded spot to myself. My next thought was echoing even louder: I am in the middle of nowhere with nothing but large animals!

The sun wavered on the horizon but the watering hole remained visible from my vantage point. I watched as a single black rhino lumbered down to the water's edge. His small mouth slurped noisily. In the hushed dusk a herd of zebras reluctantly appeared from out of the golden grass. One young male distanced himself from the others and pawed the muddy edge of the water hole. Within minutes the magnificent orange sun sank below the horizon. All seemed peaceful. A rustling from the dry grass set the zebras into flight in an instant. The young zebra was mere seconds behind his herd. The distance was enough for two female lions to cut him off from escape. One lioness leapt on the zebra's hindquarters. The other bit the air from his throat, cutting off his high-pitched primeval scream. With the two lionesses holding fast to the twitching carcass, several others moved in to share the kill.

In the fading light, I could just make out the billowing manes of the King of the Plains. I was spooked and hypnotized. While telling myself that this was an acceptable moment in the cycle of life, never had I felt more vulnerable. For over one hundred nights straight I had camped in Africa. Only at this moment did I realize the difference between camping on the side of a road and camping alone by a remote watering hole, feet away from a pride of feeding lions. I made a small fire for safety and tried to relax. Peering into the darkness, I saw my fire reflected in a pair of small lime-green eyes. To avoid further eye contact I draped the rain tarp over my tent. Pretending there was safety under the thin nylon, I scurried into my tent and listened. A few hours before dawn I heard the laughter of hyenas chasing away the lions, who were gorged on zebra meat. Then, enormous hyena jaws crunched through bones to reach the marrow.

At dawn, new sounds. With trepidation, I left my tent and saw buzzards playing what looked like a game of tag with hyenas. Chewing my own scrap of jerky, I began a speedy breakdown of my camp. At the watering hole stood a huge kudu with wildly twisting horns and white stripes. Before I could swallow my next bite, he tossed his mighty head and was gone. For me, this striking antelope will always represent Africa. Then I began my long, anxious walk back to the road. To bolster my courage, I sang in my loudest baritone voice. Never has Italian opera been so murdered. My vocal acrobatics brought me safely through the tall grassland to the road and "civilization."

African Lion

9

Velcro on My Sandals

There is no road, only a foot path 180 miles long, on the thin piece of land between Panama and Colombia. This path divides Central America from South America and is known as the Darien Gap. It is a wild trail used by traders, drug smugglers and refugees and is exploited by bandits and Colombian leftist guerrillas.

The Darien Gap is something I had always wanted to walk and it took me 20 years to build up the confidence and courage to do it. I court love, beauty and danger because they are the few things that make me feel most alive. The Darien Gap is most certainly dangerous. Nobody I knew had ever walked it. If you had a passport you would take a plane or a boat and go around it. From what I had heard, it seemed that everyone traveling along this path had a dark past, was desperate, or was running from something.

To begin the journey I chartered a ride up the Balsa River with a commercial riverboat captain. A little way up the Balsa River this captain would trade his goods of machetes, cooking pots, salt, sugar and tobacco for plantains and palm oil harvested by the Chocó natives. Then the captain would go a few days down river to a market town where he would sell the plantains, palm nuts and boat. Then he would put the engine and gas cans on the roof of a bus, come home and start the process all over again by making a new dugout canoe.

Camped out on the beach, I reflected on the fascinating geological story of this area. The narrow part of Panama rose out of the sea five million years ago to connect North and South America. This barrier created both the Atlantic Ocean and the Pacific Ocean, which dramatically changed global weather patterns. No longer did warm currents pass through the continents and provide rainfall for West Africa's rain forests. This created the major change of West Africa's rain forest into the dry savannah it is today. With the lack of rain the old-growth forests died and forced the monkeys out of the trees to survive in the grassland of the newly formed savannah. These monkeys had to start walking upright to see over the tall grass. This was the first link between monkey and *Homo sapiens* - Man the Thinker. Thank you, Panama!

Over the course of a few days I watched the captain finish constructing the boat that was to take us up river. Thirty feet long, four feet wide and the result of a month's hard labor, the boat was hand-hewn from a massive, old-growth tree. Reassured by the sight of a 50-horsepower Yamaha engine and two gas cans hidden away under a tarp, I sensed and hoped this guy was for real. I looked forward to making the journey with a new friend. But, to be honest, if the captain hadn't finished the canoe, I would have been happy. I was not just scared about this part of my journey; I was terrified!

When it came time to begin our adventure, it took 10 locals with poles to launch this beached whale of a boat. The captain's old engine started on the second pull. With only 40 pounds of salt, 50 pounds of sugar, 20 gallons of palm oil, a few pans and a dozen machetes, the boat seemed massively oversized for its cargo.

The morning after our arrival to the first Chocó village, I helped the captain load his canoe with plantains, reluctantly said good-bye, then walked alone 15 miles down the trail deeper into the Darien. In this cradle of civilization I found the next unspoiled Chocó village. The people I encountered were so tiny that the average height of the men was just to my shoulder. Both the men and the women wore their hair long with short bangs. The women were bare breasted with grass skirts, while the men wore loincloths. Tattoos were very common among both sexes. The children seemed to have a lot of time to swim and play. Except for jaguar and panther teeth worn around their necks for protection, the children were naked. The Chocó were cautious yet friendly toward me. This tribe

50

had encountered their share of outlaws but had seen few or no adventure travelers so deep in the Darien.

The clan chief invited me to sleep in his family's round house situated 12 feet off the ground. In the evening the ladder was pulled in for protection from the big cats, then the family of 10 settled in for their evening meal. The peach palms that fringed the village provided the staples of the Chocó diet. From the fruit, they made oil, beer and bread. From the sap, they made wine. That night, they shared with me their delicacy: smoked heart of peach palm. I shared my hummus, and I remember their fascination with the Velcro on my sandals. The Chocó did not speak any Spanish so communication was non-verbal, but a nod is a nod and a smile is a smile in any language. I woke up the following morning to the sound of a hungry crying baby. It was a beautiful house, a happy home!

A young man, perhaps 20 years old, took me on a hunting expedition that morning. I was sporting my new loincloth, which I had bartered for with two Power Bars. A white guy wearing only a loincloth and sandals must have been quite a sight. Next to naked, I was getting eaten alive by mosquitoes, and all I could think of was the risk of malaria. We were hunting for howler monkeys. It is not difficult to find these monkeys because they howl and don't move. My companion carried a very old, incredibly rusty and dangerous-looking rifle. I was more concerned for his safety than for that of a monkey he might shoot. After a few hours of walking we followed the unmistakable roar to a band of howler monkeys. My new native friend rested the gun on a sapling to steady his aim, and using just one bullet from the very few he carried, shot a monkey in the chest. The 40-pound male dropped out of a tree like a stone.

We gutted the monkey right there in the jungle. My young guide cut off the tail and laughing, put it around his neck. We built a bonfire and threw the monkey on it—head, hair and all. The smell of the burning hair was repulsive. It was an odor that my senses completely rejected. Thankfully we walked upwind of the fire in search of wild plantains. A few hours later, with the cooked monkey and plantains strung on a pole, we shouldered the heavy load and made the two-hour trek back to the village. My native friend was small and strong. Back in the village the tribe had gathered in excitement. They laughed at my hairy legs, which were covered with mosquito bites, and the women were concerned about the welt that the pole had left on my shoulder. Mothers will always be mothers!

The women cooked the plantains in palm oil. As the honored guest, I was the first to eat. I shook the monkey's hand, twisted the forearm off at the elbow and began gnawing on it. It was disgusting in a crazy, cannibalistic way, but I expressed approval with a big smile on my face. The men selected their pieces, and then the women and children tore into it. The feast was on! Grinning like leprechauns with charred skin stuck in everyone's teeth was a sight that I will never forget. It was an incredible meal in the best setting with fried plantains for dessert followed by a swim with the kids.

The next day my hunting friend walked south with me for about an hour. As we strolled along, he pointed out the massive primordial nut trees that surrounded his village. He indicated that his ancestors had been cultivating this area for generations. Small fields cleared by slash-and-burn gave way to beans, maize, manioc and squash, while other fields were reclaimed by the jungle and would be cultivated in years to come. So much was said with so few words. With a warm embrace, we parted the best of friends.

Chocó woman

10
Native Roots

In the early 1980s, back in the States, I was paying Dr. Ladi a dollar a day to stay in his wobbly old barn. I promised him to try to keep it standing with cables, beams, concrete and roofing. Set in the middle of the meadow, this long-forgotten 1777-era barn was once the heartbeat of his farm.

In this hand-hewn New England classic I created my transportation museum. With an airless paint sprayer I could paint huge structures very quickly. When neighbors wanted to sell their farm, I offered to paint their barn and relieve them of their unwanted treasures. My girlfriend at the time, Elizabeth, called it 'painting for pillage.' The lighter stuff went on the second-story hayloft: antique wagons, carriages, sleighs, and my bicycle collection. Down below sat a '46 Chevy truck, a '56 Chevy four door, a '72 Kharmann-Ghia convertible, a '68 Dodge Lodge van, a '72 Honda CB 350, and a 1972 60/5 BMW motorcycle. My prize was the 1948 Alden sloop, which I renamed after my grandmother, Yvonne. I was Hector the Collector and my man cave was, in my mind, the coolest hangout in town.

The wind blew through my barn, as did the bats and the sparrows. Elizabeth changed the linen and mosquito net with every weekend visit. Our huge antique bed was precariously perched in the loft. My brother Chris had lent me his collection of 18 lanterns. When lit at night, they gave the illusion that the bed actually floated in the hayloft. To make matters weirder, if you rolled out of bed, you would land on either a car or a truck.

Every other weekend found Elizabeth and me either in the barn or her Boston apartment. When staying in the country our morning routine started with a drive to Bill's Diner. On this particular morning the gang was all there: Mark, Jay, Phil, Frid and two of my brothers, Brian and Chris. Since the barn had no plumbing or electricity, Bill's Diner served as my bathroom. That morning two things happened. First, Jay was showing Chris pictures of an old mill he was trying to buy in Vermont. It was literally hanging over a waterfall. Chris gave me a hopeful look, as we had been looking to move our house painting business out of town. That was the beginning of our business in Vermont for the next eight summers. Next, Brian told me to phone my cousin Cathy as soon as possible because she wanted me to work on the sailboat *Shenandoah* for two weeks. I used to work on this old topsail, square-rigged schooner and Captain Douglas desperately needed a galley rat. That was to be one of the hardest jobs I have ever experienced: 16 hours a day in a tiny, coal-fired kitchen on a 128-foot schooner, feeding 40 people.

I have never seen the captain so happy to see me. On the tenth day of sailing we anchored in Nantucket, home to movie stars, millionaires and fishermen, and I got the day off. This amazing old whaling island is well known as the summer home to America's elite. My great-uncle Al picked me up at the dock, and we had a wonderful day. This little Frenchman was larger than life: 90 years old and still driving the biggest Cadillac known to come out of Detroit. He came to this island in his mid-20s as its first state trooper, driving a new Indian motorcycle. Great-uncle Al introduced me to his friends, millionaires and fishermen alike.

In his Caddy we whipped around the island and he showed me his big painting projects, as he had been a painting contractor in his latter years. He showed me massive wooden hotels that he and his crew had painted. We ate lunch at one of his favorite golf clubs. He was an honorary member of all of the clubs on the island, having multiple golf trophies in every clubhouse.

That night, after sundowners on Al's front porch, we talked of travel, sailing and his great life on the island. Our family has long heard the whispers of our native lineage. I finally got up my sundowner courage and asked him about the Native American side of our family. This subject has never been fully understood and was at risk of being lost with the passing of his generation. He knew only that we had Native American roots that came from somewhere out in Alberta, Canada. Our ancestors then moved back east to Quebec and eventually made their way to Fall River, Massachusetts.

This insight sparked some later research on my part and here is the most probable scenario I have come up with: My great-great-grandfather was a young Frenchman who took passage sailing across the Atlantic, most likely on a boat similar to the *Shenandoah*. He must have had some money because he continued on out west to Alberta. Many of the Frenchmen of that era ended up as loggers in French Quebec or Maine. In the mid-1800s many Frenchmen went out west and became trappers, selling pelts to supply the huge demand for fur in Europe. At that time, many French men married native women and employed the men in her family to help work the trap lines in the foothills of the Canadian Rockies.

Two months after the sailing trip I was spending time with Al's sister, my dear grandmother, Yvonne Giblin. This elegant woman in her late 80s allowed me to take her on a four-hour canoe journey down my favorite river, which meanders behind my parents' house in Florida and is the same river on which early Tarzan movies were filmed. Like my mom, Yvonne was up for anything. Her eyesight was amazing; that day on the river she was often the first one to see the teeming wildlife: birds, raccoons, deer, turtles and alligators. Being a delicate family subject, I asked her, as I did Uncle Al, what she knew of our Native American relations and history in Canada. Unfortunately for the family's historical record, my grandmother knew less than her brother, and this part of our family history may remain a mystery forever more.

11
Five Punches

I left Venice abruptly with a swollen face and a bit pissed off. Taking punches to the head is not the best way to be woken up. To be fair, for nearly a week I had been sleeping in a random boatman's gondola hidden under a tarp. But five punches to the head? Living on $15 a day can be tough: no safety from the street, no shower, no respect; you're often seen as homeless. Between the rats as big as cats and the macho boat-boys it was time to change the channel. Still, to leave such an incredible city under a dark cloud was a drag.

Little has changed in Venice in 200 years. The water streets still hear the cry of boatmen and the footsteps of pedestrians on stone bridges. The only engines heard are those of the cargo boats that supply the town with goods and the water-buses that ferry passengers.

Today the Veneto region stretches from the flat river plains of Venice to the Dolomite Mountains. In my pack I had a chalk-bag, harness and shoes, anticipating some of the best rock-climbing in the world. Partying with the local climbing community was an Italian experience of wine, women and song. We climbed hundred-foot sandstone columns created by erosion with a massive boulder crowning each column.

Hitchhiking in Italy really does suck. You could die out there. So when a cute couple in love took me home for the weekend, gifting me a shower and a load of clean laundry, it was the best thing ever. I camped in their small garden in Bologna. In the markets of this charming town I saw huge wheels of Parmesan cheese. Following my nose down a back alley, I stumbled across a 500-year-old curing house. Practicing my broken Italian, I complimented the owner on his country and the samples he was offering. He realized I was a poor backpacker and offered me a huge slab of his smoky ham. What an incredible feast! A few fountains away lies an amazing university, and as I was munching my ham in front of the spraying fountains, I gazed at the most beautiful Italian girls running to their next class. I do love this country.

On the final leg of my month in Italy I headed south towards Rome. On Thursday the weather had turned really wet and hitching became miserable. Friday found me still miles from Rome. On Saturday I was depressed; it was still a cold rain with no rides in sight. Being wet for three days had broken my Italian high, and homesickness was creeping in. My last ride had dropped me off in a bad place with no shoulder for the next car to pull over. Cold and dispirited, I walked for hours, feeling the spray of every passing car. Finally, an old beat-up Fiat bumped up over the curb, flashing its emergency lights and beeping the horn. I ran up to the best ride of this trip.

Maria and Maggie, a mother and daughter, were coming back from their cousin's birthday party. Maggie was seven years old and gave me a toothless smile from the backseat with party glitter adorning her cheeks. Maria, equally flushed with sparkles, laughed as she ground the car into gear and slammed back into traffic. Maria translated while her daughter bombarded me with questions. I told her of my long, frustrating journey to Rome. We laughed as Maggie messily fed me birthday cake from the backseat. These Italian beauties were food to my soul, and I was completely infatuated.

Maria said that the women in Italy have to be strong because of the 50 percent divorce rate. She told me that she had read that 80 percent of divorced Italian men move within a kilometer of their mothers, visiting regularly for cooking and laundry services.

We were still several hours north of Rome when Maria pulled over and jumped out and ran into a market. She was gone at least 10 minutes and when she came back she told me that this was where she must drop me off. Tears mingled with sparkles and cake crumbs as we said goodbye on the sidewalk. When I turned to leave, Maria handed me a train ticket to Rome. Before I could protest, she jumped into her dilapidated Fiat and was gone.

Standing in the rain, I was an emotional wreck and cried for at least 10 minutes, trying to get myself together. I hadn't realized she had stopped behind the train station. Inquiring within, I found out the 45-dollar ticket from Maria put me in Rome at seven that evening. This day began as one of the worst hitching days of my life. I walked for five hours, hating the Italians with every passing car drenching me. Then, a slice of magic happened. This poor single mom and her beautiful daughter in a beat-up Fiat filled me with their love and gifted me a very expensive train ticket.

The first thing I remember coming out of Rome's central train station was a massive display of fireworks. It felt like Rome was commemorating my arrival rather than the beginning of their 2000th-year Jubilee! The rain had stopped, and I followed the fireworks to St. Peter's Basilica, which Michelangelo graced with his magic touch in the 16th century. As the fireworks showered St. Peter's stone dome, I saw Pope John Paul II speak to a huge crowd. It seemed as though the whole town was under construction for the 2000 Jubilee, and I needed to find a place to camp before the crowds dispersed. I walked several blocks and in the dark climbed the scaffolding of an office building. I was physically and emotionally exhausted and soaked to the bone. I made a nest on this precarious roost and immediately fell asleep on the two-foot-wide plank.

Early the next day, I stashed my pack in a green garbage bag next to an empty trash bin and headed back to St. Peter's. I had fine brick dust stuck to my body and clothes from head to toe from the night before and was a sight to behold. Even the men sweeping up last night's party stopped to stare.

A line was forming on the steps of the basilica. Curious about the event, I scanned the crowd, looking for someone who might speak English. I spotted a shiny middle-aged woman, who turned out to be from Denmark. Ana informed me that the line was for Pope John Paul II, who was giving a special Mass. She was fascinated by my night's accommodations and my mode of transportation. Ana knew Rome very well and told me a brief history of the city, then gave me her map and offered suggestions for places to visit. She used her handkerchief soaked in her drinking water to clean my face and hands. I bought her an espresso and again, in vain, we attempted to brush off my dust-covered polyester clothes.

Ana's cell phone rang and when she hung up, she told me, "My angel has been talking to your angel, and she wants me to give you an extra ticket that has just become available." Wow, now I had a ticket for the grand reopening of St. Peter's Basilica, for which the Pope himself would do the honors! In attendance would be 200 cardinals, 500 bishops, 500 nuns and 200 select laypeople, and somehow I was to be among them!

My ragged appearance was magnified by the upscale dress of the other attendees of this event. Ana and I tried again, unsuccessfully, to wipe the brick dust off my wet clothes. Ana met up with her group, introduced me, and after I apologized again for my appearance, we went our separate ways. I did not look like I belonged anywhere near this event and among these honored guests.

As if directed by a higher power, I was ditched by the middle-aged white women, but then found myself next to a group of a dozen African nuns. Who better equipped and less insulted by a very dusty traveler? One of the nuns had four tattoos of the crucifix on her cheeks, chin and forehead. She turned out to be my favorite nun with her high spirits and good energy. These African nuns distinguished themselves from the other guests. They were laughing and crying and jumping up and down like schoolgirls at a rock concert. It was great!

The Pope spoke for three and a half hours in seven different languages. The colorful regalia of the cardinals and bishops were woven into the fabric of this profound ceremony. Only John Paul was dressed in brilliant white. As the Pope exited, I heard a woman saying in Spanish, "We love you, Papa." Tears again began to flow. The previous week had tried my faith, but with all these angels carrying me on their wings, love was once more restored in my heart.

12
Hepatitis A

In 1995 Cambodia had recently been opened up to travelers, and I was stunned by its condition. The raging 20-year civil war had left this beautiful country in tatters. My initial impression of the population was that they were also broken. I did not speak the language, and these shy people were hard to read.

My first stop was the sprawling empire of Angkor Wat, the largest religious site in the world and the heart and soul of Cambodia. Eighth-century ruins show the influence of India and Java in its intricate sandstone carvings. Angkor Wat's colossal proportions rival those of the Great Wall of China. Traveling by bicycle, I couldn't see it all in a week. The empire was abandoned to the jungle for centuries, so most of it is engulfed in a web of roots. In spite of the deterioration, I felt its attempt at being heaven on earth.

Later, I spent one month on a rented motorcycle. Because active land mines were still a huge problem, I was very cautious about staying on the road. To turn around on a small country lane I would get off my bike and make a five-point turn, in order to avoid the shoulder. I watched a farmer use his herd of goats to detect landmines in his field. Taking a cue from the locals, I camped close to the people and their animals, which had established well-beaten paths. I tiptoed through the hidden hazards of warfare.

A dusty month of traveling the mountainous countryside took me through many 'killing fields.' Mounds of human skulls and bones were all that remained from the genocide of the civil war. It left me numb to behold the magnitude of the death toll. How could this have happened?

In 1975 the Khmer Rouge took control and killed 20 percent of Cambodia's total population. An estimated 1.4 to 2 million Cambodians were executed, starved or worked to death. The Khmer Rouge had a slogan: "To spare you is no profit; to destroy you is no loss." The citizens adopted a survival philosophy: think no original thoughts, do nothing to stand out, and speak only when necessary. From 1979 to the late 1990s, the guerillas burned a path through Cambodia, heavily landmining the countryside and sabotaging the railway system.

With a couple of days left on the rental of my motorcycle, I decided to take a rail ride on a norry. A norry is a bamboo platform about the dimensions of a king-size bed. It is set on top of two independent tank axles scavenged from the war. The Cambodians constructed these 'bamboo trains,' powered by 5 hp engines and held together by gravity. To move down the track, the driver pulls the motor backwards, causing tension on the rubber belt that rotates around the front axle, giving it propulsion in a rattling, clackety way. Constantly swapping out parts and exchanging engines, axles and bamboo platforms, no two norries are identical. Such was the ingenuity of the Cambodians.

France built a rail system in 1920 that crossed Cambodia. In 1953 Cambodia won its independence from France and was left with the railway system, which was quite the worse for wear. Today the tired train breaks down regularly on the damaged tracks. So slow is its pace that children can easily jog alongside it. This system is so decrepit that the only functioning train left in the country takes 16 hours to make the journey from Battambang to Phnom Penh, which is only a five-hour trip by bus.

The age-old train station at Bat Doeng consists of a few bamboo homes at a tiny intersection. There was a man with a prosthetic leg sitting on the tracks and young women holding an impromptu market selling vegetables. I watched the beggar monks chanting their morning prayers while I sat in the shade eating *bai sach chrouk*, grilled, marinated pork over rice.

I struck a deal for passage for myself and the motorcycle with a shirtless old man who had a huge tattoo of the ruins of Angkor Wat on his chest. He was the cheaper of the two norry drivers. My motorcycle had to be laid down in order to travel on the bamboo train. The norry driver happily siphoned my gas into his tank.

I watched as passengers slowly filled our norry platform, paying the equivalent of 50 cents. The passengers thought nothing of camping comfortably with their gear right on top of my motorcycle. Tangles of legs, bags, chickens and children made up our cargo on this undersized makeshift rail car. I sat next to a man with sun-baked skin and the permanent squint of fading eyesight. A Muslim woman in a headscarf, gently cradling her eggs, was pressed up against me and the tire of my bike.

We were going about as fast as one could run. The 30 miles from Bat Doeng to Trapange Leuk was an all-day affair. The movement created a breeze, which kept the intense heat and humidity at a tolerable level. But when we came to a slow stop for an oncoming lumber norry, I instantly began sweating. The passing norry, twice our size and heavily laden with newly cut lumber, had the right of way. With no fuss, every passenger and the lumbermen quickly disassembled our norry and helped reassemble it on the other side of the lumber norry. Teamwork, muscle and the many hands made light work of this task. In what seemed like 10 minutes our norry was back on track. The passengers resumed their positions and we were off again. What might have been an inconvenient nuisance to anyone else was an everyday occurrence to the resilient Cambodians. By sunset we reached the end of the line.

After navigating a month of precarious riding, I returned the rented motorcycle and happily hitched big trucks to the town of Kratie, where the mighty Mekong River flows out of Laos. The riverbanks were dotted with colorful houseboats. I had decided to head downriver for a few weeks. I purchased a broken teak rowboat for 20 dollars. I did my best to stymie the finger-wide crack in the bottom of my boat with a patch of tar.

On the Mekong River I was in search of adventure and the ever-elusive river dolphin. I had barely launched my craft before the water was seeping in, ankle-deep. I was grateful for the protection my plastic garbage bag offered my pack. My paddle was no more than a broken plank found on the riverbank. It was wonderful to see the normally reticent locals have a good laugh at my expense; a white tourist in a worn-out straw hat bailing his boat after every 20 paddles. No matter how I tried to prevent the leak, it only seemed to get worse. Unfortunately, the locals also use the river as a toilet and though I eventually got used to the smell, hygienically speaking I should not have been in this water.

Day after day, I floated down the beautiful Mekong and camped on its banks at night. I never did see the elusive river dolphin but I heard it tastes delicious. On the seventh day, I felt a bit achy and feverish and hadn't slept too well. On the eighth day, I woke up extremely ill, abandoned the boat and dragged myself to the nearest cheap hotel by the riverbank.

Wracked with uncontrollable shivers and fever, I found a beautiful young maid at the hotel who took pity on me. In spite of our language barrier I had no choice but to completely trust her. I gave her all my Cambodian money and then she helped me secretly bury my money belt in a secluded spot outside my door in the hotel's garden. With the very last of my strength, I wrote in big letters in magic marker on my room wall: Kevin McNally 3/6/60 USA. Christ, I thought I was going to die there! The maid urgently ran for her uncle who was a taxi man. He literally carried me to his makeshift, three-wheeled motorcycle taxi and took me directly to the hospital.

Blood work determined that I had hepatitis A. I was shocked because years earlier I was inoculated for hepatitis. Back in my room, in a semi-conscious state, I wondered about this with as much clarity as I could and then it came to me. Years ago, I was on the Chad border in Africa, searching for an overland route to Sudan. It was time for my six-month hepatitis booster. I vaguely remember standing in line at a rundown local hospital full of sick people and watching a cat lick blood off the floor. I was so disgusted that I left and thought I'd wait until I got to Senegal for the booster. I forgot! This recollection of events did not make my sickness any more tolerable. After three weeks of a coconut milk and 90-pill-per-day diet, I made friends with my liver again and was able to continue my trip, though it would take me another year to fully recover.

One of my biggest regrets was forgetting to follow up on that booster shot. Here I was, halfway around the world and had no choice but to completely trust strangers to keep me alive. Though I was defenseless and deadly sick, all of my money, dignity and health were restored due to the kindness and can-do spirit of the Cambodians. They showed me how to rebound from dire circumstances with optimism and resourcefulness, something at which Cambodians are well practiced.

Mountain monastery, Cambodia

13
Antarctic Galley Rat

Years before this trip, I had hitchhiked all the way down to the very tip of South America to the town of Ushuaia, the gateway to Antarctica. It was there that I first saw the *Europa*, an old square-rigged sailing ship. It was built in 1911 and is an impressive 56-meter steel-hull. At that time I had no extra money and promised myself that I would not return here without stacks of cash to visit my last remaining continent on this beautiful sailing ship.

A dozen years later, I was back in Ushuaia, stalking the captain and crew of the *Europa*. They had just returned from a three-week trip and were partying in one of the restaurants in town. I nervously went up and asked the captain if he had time to talk. The smile fell from his face and he asked, "How much time?"

"Just a few minutes, captain." I replied.

I steered him to a dark corner near the bathroom and showed him an apple-sized wad of bills amounting to $5,000, one-third of what his paying passengers would be giving him. I quickly rattled off the names of some of the square-rig schooners I had worked on back in New England. I asked him if I could be a paying crew member. Not only would I pay for my passage, I would also work and sleep anywhere. I explained that I had hitched down from Colombia and that Antarctica was my last continent. I gave him the 100-country rap, but I could see he was losing interest. As the captain headed back to his table, he asked exactly how much money I had and told me to be packed and waiting early in the morning in two day's time, but that he couldn't promise anything. He went back to his table full of friends, drinks and food. Nobody acknowledged my leaving, and I felt sure my chances of getting aboard were minimal. I walked through the town of Ushaia back to my graveyard camp. Fat, Gor-Tex-wearing tourists were shopping and contrasted greatly with the wiry, tanned crew of the *Europa* I had just seen partying with the captain.

Two days later, I was at the dock at the agreed-upon time. Nobody acknowledged my presence. By 10 o'clock they were ready to pull the dock lines, and I was almost in tears when Captain Case and Phoebe, the New Zealand cook, came off and I jumped to attention. Captain Case asked me my name and introduced me to Phoebe, my new boss. "You'll be sleeping in the galley, working long hours, and don't be a nuisance to the paying guests," barked the captain as he discreetly took my $5,000. I was ecstatic as I got my 'welcome aboard hug' from Phoebe and for the first time the crew acknowledged me with smiles and a nod. I proudly boarded with my well-worn pack.

Finally, a dream come true. I was going around the Horn in a massive hundred-year-old sailing ship. The rusty *Europa* was well worn and in desperate need of a refit. On our sail out of the harbor this ancient ship was an amazing contrast to the converted Russian icebreakers that were also making the journey to Antarctica. Our crew was mostly Dutch, and the passengers were a mix of scientists and wealthy adventure seekers. The winds were light, and we made a slow passage across to the Palmer Peninsula of Antarctica. The Antarctic summer, with its long days, gave me time to help sail this old tired beauty. Everyone seemed to be very appreciative of the food and hospitality from Phoebe's small galley. The continent was so incredibly bleak and inhospitable and completely devoid of humanity that it magnified every luxury onboard our self-sufficient floating expedition.

On the twentieth day, we slowly sailed up a scenic fjord among majestic, glacier-blue icebergs. Swimming penguins were like little missiles leading the way at the bow. The hue of the midnight sun glanced off the ice in screaming red luminosity. A pod of humpback whales breached, bubble feeding on the krill now plentiful in the Antarctic summer. Captain Case ordered the old vessel into irons, and we side-slipped up to these mammoth creatures. As we slowed, I climbed up the rigging and shimmied out on the lower yardarm for the best possible position. From 30 feet above, I made direct eye contact with one of the massive creatures, which had his head six feet out of the water. I was so close to it that I could actually feel and smell the whale's warm fishy breath. His slippery black skin gleaming in the last rays of the sun was fascinating. In one of the most far-flung regions of the world, this gentle giant appeared to be as captivated by my presence as I was by his. That moment will never ever leave me.

Antarctica

14

Jesus on the Dashboard

My earliest recollection of great adventure is summers with my family sailing around the Thousand Islands region of the St. Lawrence River along the New York/Canadian border. With 1,800 islands to explore, I uncovered everything from snakes, wild pigs, and deer to abandoned boathouses and million-dollar mansions. It all depended on where the wind blew us on any given day. To a carefree nautical boy, it was like sailing away to different worlds.

Our 30-foot sailboat, *Aquarius*, was tiny when it was packed with a family of nine. In tune with the times we were long-haired, hippie tree-huggers. My rite of passage came at the age of seven, when my mother allowed me to leave the safety of the boat and go camping with my two older brothers. My father would drop anchor off the leeward side of one of the islands, and my brothers and I would take our pup tent, sleeping bags, hot dogs and matches in the dingy and row ashore to freedom camp. Mom and Dad were still within shouting range, but during those nights I believed myself to be wholly emancipated from them.

In the highlands of Guatemala, especially around Lake Atitlan, I was reminded of those adventures and of a sense of community. Lake Atitlan is the largest lake in Central America and floats in the sky a mile above sea level, relying on three 10,000-foot majestic volcanoes to hold gravity at bay. *Atitlan* is a Mayan word that translates as 'the place where the rainbow gets its colors.' Even today Mayan culture and the spirit it invokes is the hidden gem of Guatemala, making this one of the most exotic destinations in the world.

Mayan culture is predominant in the lakeside communities. Panajachel is the largest town on the shores of Atitlan and has been overwhelmed throughout the years by tourists. It attracted many hippies in the 1960s. The 'ugly '80s' refers to its civil war, which caused all the foreigners to leave. By the time I arrived in 1990, visitors were beginning to return.

The first time I walked around this lake, I was astounded at the dozen or so villages surrounded by such natural beauty. The shy Mayan people are friendly, colorful and welcoming to strangers. Every village has its own unique language and dress. The women weave their own clothing using a back-strap loom. I was buying up beautiful old hand-made embroidered textiles. The volcanic mountainside is dotted with the red berries of the coffee trees. Harvest season is the busiest time of the year for the residents, and the smell of the sour discarded husk of the coffee beans permeated every village. Throughout the day the farmers raked and dried the beans on huge sheets of black plastic. Children were on vacation from school to help harvest Guatemala's main export and the Mayan's only cash crop. In the absence of a road, it took me seven days to slowly walk around the lake.

The following summer, to save money for an Asian trip, I painted a church and a huge mill that overhung a river in Vermont. The owners couldn't find any other painter willing to risk life and limb. At the very end of my painting season, my leg was injured when I was run off the road while motorcycle riding. I ended up collecting $7,000 from the accident. Because of the injury, I changed my Asia plans and limped back to Lake Atitlan to buy a piece of property with this new-found wealth.

I found my lakeside paradise in the small village of San Marco, an 800-year-old pueblo with a population of about 400 Cachikel Mayans. Living among the farming community of this tiny village was an intoxicating experience. While all of the natives lived in the village above, the foreigners built right on the lake. I kept busy landscaping my sloping property using natural rock from the area to create stonewall terraces and tried in vain to keep the neighbor's cattle from eating my recently planted fruit trees. A beautiful snaking stone path starting at the lake's edge cut right up the middle of the property and led to my future home site.

Towards the end of the winter, I was having second thoughts about homesteading here or, for that matter, anywhere. Returning to the same place, as beautiful as it was, was throwing down roots that felt too deep. For the first time in my life, instead of owning a boat and borrowing the land, I owned the land and was borrowing a boat. I felt sure that life still had too many surprises for this much domestication.

It was then that I came down with a bad infection on my leg known around the lake as the 'dirty hippie disease.' I took the 90-minute boat ride into the town of Panajachel, hoping to catch a bus to Chimaltenango to address this medical condition. With foreigners from every corner of the globe, Panajachel is a real "Hippie United Nations." I saw my San Marco neighbor Paloma and her tiny mutt on a sidewalk outside a European bakery, playing her guitar for loose change. Paloma means "dove" in Spanish. While Paloma told people she was 20 years old, I knew she was only 16. She was a half-Mexican, half-French perfect racial mix of exotic beauty, and people fell silent when she strummed her 12-string guitar. Well aware of her beauty, Paloma acted years older than her age and paid for very little out of her own pocket for anything.

Paloma had a massive pimple on her cheek, which made her right eye look swollen. When I teased her about it, she said, "I've got an even bigger one on my leg." Lifting her hippie skirt ever so slightly, she showed me a welt the size of a large chicken egg. "That's exactly what I have," I told her as I rolled back my bandage, "It's called staph." By now my leg was swollen and painful with a hot throbbing burn. I knew the core of the infection was deep, and I was anxious to seek treatment. I told Paloma I was on my way to Chimaltenango to see a doctor. In a second, she put her guitar to bed, scooped up the pooch and said, "Let's go."

I had planned to take the bus, but she insisted on hitchhiking since she had no money. With a beautiful girl, we were bound to make our destination in the four hours before my 2:30 p.m. doctor's appointment. The first three rides were in the back of Toyota trucks and the warm breeze and scenery were fabulous. Paloma played Beatles tunes in Spanish and Mayan, which our fellow Mayan passengers found wildly funny. She was one in a million, a teenage runaway speaking five languages, making life on the road look fun and easy. She loved hanging out with her older brothers, as she put it, allowing her to be even wilder and more spontaneous.

Our fourth ride was a descent into hell! The driver was your classic 35-year-old macho trucker from the capital. The only reason he picked us up was because of my gorgeous French companion. He hated the fog and he hated the people of the highlands. "Shitty weather and stupid village people," he summed it up in Spanish. The interior of his truck was a virtual theatre of religious icons, ornaments, and trinkets, all outlined in smoke-stained orange shag carpet. Overloaded with what must have been 20,000 pounds of steel rebar, he barreled around the steep switchbacks, making the cab sway uncomfortably beneath the weight. Every sharp turn that made our driver apply the brakes lit up the red eyes of Jesus on the dashboard. This plastic crucified Jesus was tripping me out. Every time the driver shifted, he took advantage of the tight quarters in the cab by touching Paloma's naked knee. The fog enveloped the high points of the mountains, making me feel even more claustrophobic. As if the driving conditions were not tough enough, Paloma made it worse by lighting a joint. Our 'cowboy' was a hard-drinking city boy who had probably smoked very little in his life. Paloma blazed up and had the cab stinking in a puff. She passed it to the driver and he drew a hard hit, coughing until his eyes watered. She passed it to me and to her dismay I threw it out the window.

The fog outside was thickening. I knew that our driver, with an oversized load, was stoned because his driving skills were deteriorating as fast as the weather. His turns were becoming wider, occasionally hitting the soft shoulder of the road. He failed to slow down and smashed into a speed bump through a small village. This was turning into a real shit show. At an elevation of nearly 8,000 feet, we were still climbing through the dense cloud forest. The visibility dropped to about 30 feet, and it was difficult to discern what was around the bend. The kaleidoscope of cracks in the wet windshield made matters even worse. The windshield wipers were third-world terrible and further added to the distortion.

Paloma was humming to the mindless tunes she kept trying to dial in on the radio and seemed oblivious to the peril. Convinced that this steel cage was going to be my coffin, I was experiencing my own personal shower of nervous perspiration. I put my daypack between my body and the windshield, disregarding the Mother Mary shrine on the orange shag dash and braced my feet for the impact I expected at any moment. It seemed like hours before the altitude finally began to drop. Our truck, swaying beneath the overload of steel on its back, descended into Chimaltenango where we finally got out. Miraculously we made our appointment.

A couple of weeks later, I was banging in the 'For Sale' sign on my property when I saw Paloma again. She asked why I was moving on, and I explained that I had decided that owning a piece of land didn't make as much sense as owning a sailboat; land seemed too stationary. She flipped her hair, and through perfect white teeth and full lips she said in her sexiest voice, "When you buy your boat, you'll have to take me on a big long trip." "Sure," I said smiling, knowing that it would never happen.

My property on Lake Atitlan, Guatemala

15
The Australian Rodeo

I was Down Under and three months over the expiration date of my Australian tourist visa. Back in Thailand, I had purchased 10 pounds of silver bracelets with the last of my money and was hoping to resell them in Australia and New Zealand for a tidy profit. Now I had overstayed my Australian visa and was an illegal alien, selling my wares.

Western Australia is incredibly desolate. The red landscape with the blue sky has an intensity that burns into your mind. The distances are so vast it makes you feel small and, for me, it manifested a desire to make tighter emotional bonds with new friends.

In Western Australia a fellow named Pete picked me up hitchhiking. He was envious that I had so much time on my hands to explore his country. He generously purchased two of my bracelets for his mother and sister. We pulled into a station, and my new friend Pete went in to pay for fuel. I pumped the gas and checked the oil and cleaned all the windows, inside and out, ignoring the passed-out, fly-covered Aborigine on the porch. The station was self-sufficient with solar panels, a backup diesel generator and a windmill for pumping water. Pete came out of the station with a bagful of groceries, four gallons of water and two cans of cold beer.

It's difficult to describe the washboard roads of this country; the deep, closely spaced ridges permanently etched into the hard-packed dirt are endless. You have to travel at 5 mph or 55 mph to float up and over these road moguls. It is so deafening and jarring to the bones, the mind and the vehicle that you're exhausted after an hour and conversation is impossible.

Well into this trip, we passed a dead kangaroo. It was a big Red that I had heard about, probably seven feet tall in his better days. On his bloated belly was an enormous, wedge-tailed eagle. The eagle was eye level to me in the Rover and didn't fly off when we passed by in a cloud of dust.

An hour later, Pete pulled over to the side of the road and asked me to roll up the window because there was a road train coming. He was excited because I'd never seen an 'Australian Hurricane' before. Turning around, I saw a large dust cloud a half mile behind us. A Mack cab towing not one, but three, full-size trailers all together half the length of a football field roared by at 80 mph. We waited a good ten minutes for the dust to settle and visibility to return.

Two hundred miles later, at dusk, Pete announced that the farm where he worked was just up the way. He pulled over at a dry riverbed and said, "It will be a great adventure if you walk up this riverbed and look for gold nuggets. A full day's walk will lead you to a cliff that has little water but lots of wildlife." With a handshake, a few groceries and the three gallons of water that he had intended for me all along, Pete left me to the crimson sky.

That night I camped by the side of the road with my 25 pounds of water. The next morning, I made base camp five miles up the dry riverbed. As I was making tea on a small smoky fire, a barefoot Aborigine, sporting only shorts and a smile, walked past my camp and casually wished me a "g'day." In his hand was a burning coal, sandwiched between two pieces of moss. The rhythm of his swinging arm kept the coal alive for his next fire. It was the only thing he was carrying. He was using the dry riverbed as a road with the shade of the gum trees and soft pebbles under foot. Where was he going? Where was he coming from? The next town was 200 miles away! I had been in Australia for six months, and he was the first true bushman I had come across. I was so disappointed that he didn't join me in a cup of tea and conversation.

Later that evening at the base of the cliff I could hear the trickle of water but couldn't see it. The abundance of plants and birds was a further indication that the water source was nearby. As promised, wherever there is a little water in Western Australia, there are lots of exotic birds. Cockatoos, macaws and many other crazy colored birds I'd never seen before fluttered and flashed in the shadows of this desert oasis. Thanks to Pete's food and water, I enjoyed three days in a place very few people get to see.

After packing up my camp, I hiked back to the bridge and up onto the road where some ranchers picked me up. They were clean-cut Christian cowboys, perfectly outfitted, trailering two horses. I laid in the back of their pickup truck with a western saddle as my pillow, soaking up the smells of leather. I rode with them all the way to their destination - the rodeo.

The cowboys introduced me around and helped me get a volunteer job as a gatekeeper. I didn't have the traditional uniform of Wrangler jeans, boots and rodeo buckle. Only the rodeo clown and I were freakishly out of dress; we had similar broken straw hats and I also wore a mustard-stained long-sleeve plaid shirt, along with dress slacks and sandals. My job was to open the gates for the horse riders while keeping the cattle in the pen.

The women's barrel racing especially fascinated me. It was fashionable for the girls to lose their hat in the last stretch of the race, and one of my jobs was to return the lost hat to its rider. On Sunday I returned a hat to a 19-year-old Australian beauty. Her fresh face, honey-colored hair and blue eyes were intoxicating. As a volunteer, I followed the rodeo up the coast, and on the second weekend, I saw this beauty once again. Catherine was fascinated by my travel stories, and I was equally fascinated by her remote upbringing. Catherine told me how she longed for the city. She had spent her entire life the only child on a huge ranch with only her parents and Aboriginal ranch hands. Like other remote rancher kids, she was schooled via ham radio. That night her father came in on his helicopter. This gal was rodeo royalty in middle-of-nowhere Western Australia.

On the other side of the fence, I was invited to camp with the Aborigines. Several of us sat around a fire swapping stories. Ah, to finally be accepted by these shy people and touch the subtle cadence of their culture. Their faces looked prehistoric in the flickering flames, and I thought to myself that they must be the oldest people on the planet! Their intelligent eyes were framed by a heavy brow and bulbous nose. Our conversation was about changing times and the Sunday bull ride. On the rodeo circuit, the Aborigines weren't interested in ribbons; they were after the prize money for the bull riding, which was the last event of the weekend. One of the lanky Aboriginal teenagers with a big white smile won the bull riding prize money, and I joined the big celebration that evening in their camp. We partied around the bonfire late into the night, sparks flying up into the western sky.

While hitching my way to the next rodeo 300 miles north, I stopped at a station. As I washed the windows and made myself useful to the guy who'd picked me up, I asked the station owner what the closest city was to here. "Jakarta, mate. Jakarta, Indonesia," he replied. It was remarkable to think that the nearest city to where we were could be on another continent!

Since few of the Aborigines have licenses to drive or even know how, my new friend, a large Aboriginal matriarch,h asked me to drive a car to pick up some meat for dinner. I immediately agreed and drove to a house and picked up what turned out to be an entire quarter of a cow. The huge piece of meat was hanging in the open carport. I backed up to it and cut it loose. It was too big for the trunk to close, so I tried to keep it closed with my belt, but as I drove the meat got covered in dust. Nonetheless we had a huge feed from it and a little too much alcohol. People slept right where they fell; horse blanket in the dirt, a saddle for a pillow. Unfortunately the harmony of the evening turned hostile when a couple broke out into a serious domestic dispute. I quietly moved my camp to the other side of the fairgrounds, closer to the conservative ranchers.

The next morning I saw Catherine from a distance with her mother and father having breakfast next to their huge, air-conditioned motor home. The extremes of the contrasting lifestyles were wearing thin from my sunburnt, hungover perspective, and this dusty no-longer-wannabe cowboy longed for more balance. I had been on this overland journey for well over 400 days. In that moment I made up my mind to leave the rodeo circuit behind and headed further up the coast to the town of Broome.

16

Bone Chillers

———————

Growing up in the United States, not too far from the Canadian border, I was no stranger to cold. My first case of frostbite came at Mad River Glen Ski Area in Vermont when I was eleven years old. In conditions well below zero, with a crazy wind chill, I lost my hat when I took a fall and broke one of my skis. By the time I walked down to the lodge, my ears were crunchy frozen. The next day they hurt like hell and my earlobes were three times their normal size.

My next winter-related disaster came while skating after school on a frozen brook behind our house. Brooks are particularly precarious skating rinks: the stronger the current, the thinner the ice. When I went on my daily solo skating adventure that particular afternoon, temperatures seemed to be in the negatives, but I still managed to break through the ice and plunged to the bottom. I fought for my life against the current so as not to lose the hole I fell through, while I held my hockey stick lengthwise across my chest and broke the thin ice. It took me several tense minutes to get up and out of the river. I skated and ran the half-mile down the street, clothes frozen to my body and the new skates still on my feet. My mother put me in a cold bath and my brothers helped remove my skates and jeans. It was several hours before my hands and feet could function again.

These first two bone chillers did nothing to shake my winter wonder. However, when I was 17 years old, a winter incident in New Hampshire made a lasting impression. I had recently passed a winter survival course at the prep school I attended in the White

Mountains. My friend Rob and I decided we'd celebrate by doing some winter camping. We checked and rechecked our gear and the weather forecast, and that Friday at 9:00 a.m. under a slate-colored sky and misting rain, we hitchhiked up to Franconia Notch, a recreation area in the White Mountains. When we arrived, it was about 40 degrees, just as the weather report had predicted. We started up Mount Lafayette with crampons on our boots to grip the ice, and eventually changed to snowshoes as the snow became deeper. Summiting in six grueling hours, we were very happy with our performance.

Afterwards we built a snow cave off the north face and prepared to spend the night. The snow was thick and wet, and we made a big snow boulder to use as a front door to our cave. As we worked, the sky was clearing and the temperatures plummeted. Sometime around 5:00 p.m. we pulled out the stove and soon encountered our first problem. When we lit it, the high-pressure fuel burst a seal in the stove, spurting streams of flame throughout the snow cave and all over our gear. We turned the valve off and quickly extinguished the flames. Rob and I were both soaked with perspiration from a long day of physical activity. We really needed hot water in the form of soup and tea to hydrate and warm up. Without our stove, we had to settle for frozen cheese sandwiches and ice-cold water.

After dinner I took off my one-piece Gore-Tex alpine suit, super-gaiters and hiking boots, used them as a pillow and slipped into my winter down sleeping bag. Throughout the evening, our body heat and the conditions outside conspired against us. The melt-off from the cave walls made a slushy floor, and as the temperature outside fell below freezing, our slushy ice cave refroze. By midnight the temperature had dropped to negative 20° Fahrenheit, a 60-degree difference in eight hours. My thermal sleeping pad froze to the snow cave floor along with almost everything else we had.

By sunrise the next day, I had been shivering uncontrollably for more than five hours. Rob, somewhat delirious himself, realized I had made a big mistake. While he had left his boots on during the night, I had taken mine off. My boots were now two blocks of ice that I couldn't open, much less put on my feet. Rob looked into my desperate eyes and slowly said, "No boots, no crampons." He tried to chip our gear out of the frozen floor with his ice axe. He soon realized the futility of the effort and turned his attention to me. The wind had really kicked in, and I was well into the secondstage of hypothermia. He dressed me in my one-piece Gore-Tex, three pairs of socks and my leather overboots. Then he put his gear on.

To get off the mountain, we had to get over the summit we'd climbed the day before and down the backside of a 4,000-foot saddle. It was 8:00 a.m. and we were ready to attempt our escape. Time was of the essence. It took only 20 minutes of exposure to the cold and gusting wind to further weaken me. The snow, saturated by mist, was now a sheet of ice, and without crampons I couldn't stay on my feet.

Initially, we roped in together with a six-foot lead between us, but it quickly became evident that we needed to shorten it to two feet so Rob could more fully support my weight. When I asked him to shorten my lead, he stepped forward and accidentally put one of the blades of his crampon deep into my foot. It didn't hurt like it should have, but I knew it was bad because it took so much effort for him to separate us.

Hypothermic and losing our judgment, we made yet another major mountaineering safety mistake when Rob completely untied me while attempting to shorten the lead line again. I fell down for what must have been the fiftieth time, but untied from the lead rope I began sliding down the icy face of the mountain at an incredible pace. I finally stopped a good 200 feet down the slope and was knocked out cold; for how long I don't know. Rob trudged down and found me in a patch of scrubby hemlock. He looped a rope around my armpits and miraculously dragged me back up to the summit. Semiconscious, I was like a rag doll as he lowered me with rope down the other side of the mountain.

By the grace of God and Rob's herculean effort, we reached the road seven hours later. Rob deposited me in a snowbank and frantically tried to wave down passing motorists in the twilight. Anxiously waving two ice axes, with a balaclava fully covering his face, he wasn't getting any takers. The wind was so intense in the notch that day that Cannon Ski Area was closed and there was very little traffic. Night was falling, and we both would have died of hypothermia if not picked up! Thank God, an hour and a half later, a mother stopped and went out of her way to drop us at our school's infirmary. I spent a week there healing before returning to classes. Six weeks later, we returned to the mountain and found most of our borrowed gear.

This experience changed the way I travel. Big mountains can kill. Regardless of even careful planning, one cannot always be prepared for extreme conditions. I want to see the planet on warmer terms. Thankfully, so many of the great cultures around the world wear sandals!

Rob digging snow cave, Lafayette summit

17
The Dusty Bucket of Love

The island country of New Zealand is a hitchhiker's paradise. The native Maori live in the warmer northern region, and these friendly people have absolutely no reservations about picking up a stranger. There's a sense of well-being and safety between the native inhabitants and the tourists.

Cities worldwide deter the homeless from sleeping in parks with No Trespassing signs, fences, spiked gates and early-morning sprinklers. I always treat No Trespassing signs as a personal invitation whenever scoping out a free-camping site in the late afternoon. Wellington's Central Park in New Zealand was closed for the night, and after three attempts to throw my heavy pack over its 10-foot iron-spiked fence, I eventually succeeded. Now I had to follow. The height, texture and sharpness of the fence were all designed to mess you up. You had to get the last bit right - don't spike yourself and don't break your ankles on the way down. Behind the gardener's shed seemed as good a place as any to sleep. With no light or tent, I snuggled behind some low plants.

At crack of day I was still in the last remnants of a good dream when a torrent of freezing-cold water hit me. Bolting upright in my tiny camouflaged mummy sleeping bag, I wrestled it open and madly started collecting my gear. As the sprinkler turned and hit me for a second time, I saw three gardeners, looking like Larry, Curly and Moe, smirking, in between sips of tea. They had a fourth cup of tea ready for me.

The solution to the problem of sprinklers, I have learned, is to find the sprinkler head, secure a plastic bag over it and sleep uphill. The only problem is being able to find it the first night.

After tea with the gardeners, I headed further north out of the city limits. Later that day I came to realize that the contrast in landscapes was as extreme as the people. A new green Land Rover pulled over to pick me up, and I met one of the islanders of British descent. Mr. Ashbury was the real deal. With his ruddy cheeks, tweed cap and rubber boots, he appeared to be a true gentleman. His high-strung border collies riding in the back were overly happy to see me. He asked me to join him for afternoon tea and said his home was up the road a short distance. A gently sloping driveway led up to a spotless, whitewashed working farm on a knoll overlooking the ocean.

Mr. Ashbury introduced me to his wife, who was clearly flustered over the arrival of an unannounced and grimy guest. More English than the English, but gracious nonetheless, Mrs. Ashbury fluttered and fussed over me like a mother hen while making polite conversation. Her teeth were whiter than the pearls she was wearing. The contrast between the china and immaculate lace and my muddy shoes and mustard-stained wash-and-wear plaid shirt made me feel more than uncomfortable.

Mrs. Ashbury escorted me to an antique white Victorian chair. I tried to keep my sweaty, smelly body contained to the space allotted. I sipped tea from their best china and accepted repeated apologies from my hostess for day-old scones while politely nodding over the family photo album. Sensing our discomfort, Mr. Ashbury offered me extra rubber boots for a tour of the grounds. When the gentleman took me outside to see his farm, my visit improved immensely. I'm sure Mrs. Ashbury was as relieved as I was.

This farm, with its amazing views of pasture and sea, had the distinct feeling of some old English novel. The tour was fascinating, but I noticed the conversation was a bit one-sided as Mr. Ashbury expounded on his operation and his heritage. It was all very interesting and I'll give anybody an hour, but I was getting a crick in my neck from nodding so much. As I began discreetly sidestepping,

Mr. Ashbury surprised me when he suggested that I stay and work with him for a while. He probably thought he was doing a drifter a favor and while I appreciated the gesture, I'm not sure if he really liked me or just wanted a captive audience. These proper folks and their nervous hospitality wouldn't hear of letting me camp in their yard and their house was just too clean. I respectfully declined and with a warm handshake, heaved my well-worn pack onto my back and headed towards the road, hitching for my next ride.

A nine-passenger station wagon pulled over. The old, rusty Chevy already had a dozen people packed inside but this Maori family wouldn't refuse one more. I tried to let them off the hook by claiming that my pack and I just couldn't fit, but the driver Johnny would have none of it. Taking his belt off and demanding another from his brother, he tied my pack to the roof and slammed both belt ends in the car door while I squeezed in with two children on my lap. Stacked like pancakes, shy smiles and curious stares greeted me and when I told them my name they instantly shortened it to Kev. The kids asked me great questions and laughed at my jokes. This dusty bucket of love immediately made me feel right at home.

A dozen miles down the road, we dropped into their family farm, full of fruit and nut trees and a huge vegetable garden. The family was just returning from a five-day road trip, and one by one, large and small, they poured out of the car and immediately began attacking the new weeds in the garden, pointing out a row for me. With the trained eye of a painter, I could tell their two-story, dilapidated home hadn't been painted in generations. Plainly there wasn't any room in the house, but they offered me the sunny side of their shed to put up my tent. I couldn't have felt more at home.

A wonderful selection of fruit and nut trees twisted haphazardly throughout the yard. There were almond, apple, apricot, macadamia and hazelnut, but the prize of this small farm was a magnificent avocado tree gracing the entrance to the house. I asked if they had any animals and was told they had a few dozen laying hens that they kept down the road. Their love of traveling was the reason they couldn't be responsible for livestock. The only vehicle on the entire farm was the old station wagon with a hitch for their trailer.

While making bread with the help of the animated children, one of the mothers of this multi-family house told me about their holiday to the coast. Here in the warmth of their well-used kitchen, my muddy sandals and dirty clothes fit right in. I told them that I too, came from a large family in the States and although I travelled extensively, I usually had more time than money. They hounded me for my travel tales as if I had enough good stories to fill a lifetime. The children were fascinated and bombarded me with more questions. "Where do you sleep, Kev?," "Where do you get your food?", "Is it safe at night?", "Don't you get lonely?", etc.

Seeing that I had little money and couldn't pay my way for a night out with the adults, one of the mothers in this communal household asked if I would help her 15-year-old son, Stuart, babysit the younger children. That night after a dinner of salad, homemade bread, and avocado sandwiches, they left Stuart and me in charge and headed out for the pub. Even in the absence of a television there were plenty of games and plenty of kids to play them. There was a subtle pecking order to this brat pack co-op that they all understood. This contented clan appeared to take care of themselves.

Stuart was spellbound with the idea of cheap world travel. He was especially fascinated with Europe and was saving his money to live there. We had several conversations about hitchhiking and freedom camping throughout the week. We went over things like essential gear, and I mentioned apples and dandelion greens as wild food available in many regions of the world. We uncovered possibilities that ignited his youthful mind. Despite Stuart's adolescence or maybe because of it, his perspective redirected my outlook when he said, "Plans are useful but don't get overly attached to them. Right, Kev?" He was going to be a good traveler.

The next day the kids made even more of a mess in the kitchen by making pancakes. Johnny found out I was a painter and something of a carpenter. He had me straighten out rusty nails and replace some rotten wood. There was always a project and lots of little helpers in the wake.

Days later, the family packed a picnic lunch, piled into the rusty old Chevy and headed to the beach. A traditional Sunday outing for the Maori is collecting shells to sprinkle on their ancestors' graves while reciting prayers. The Maori believe that the spirit of the dead jump off the northern peninsula to free their souls. They are a real 'food, friends, and family' culture. The beach was beautiful and the day was perfect.

After a week, I had to devise a story to take leave of this beautiful family and head back out on the road. All 12 members came to see me off in an emotional farewell. Hugs and handshakes signaled my departure, and Johnny the proud father said to me, "Among family there are no goodbyes, Kev." They sat in their car, steaming up the windows, while waiting for me to catch my next ride. I gave a final wave to my adoptive family, knowing I would someday return. The Maori know exactly how this traveler likes to be treated: don't fuss over me and, by giving me a chore, you make me one of the clan.

Trampoline and sprinkler boys in New Zealand

18
Lifesavers

Turning travelers on to hitching gives me a thrill. In Guatemala I met a seasoned traveler named Leslie who worked as a copy editor. Leslie had never hitched before and was excited to join me on my trip south. She was amazed at how fun and easy it was to get rides standing at speed bumps on the edge of town where truckers had to slow down. One of our many rides was in an empty coffee truck, headed to the southernmost tip of El Salvador. We cleared customs in the colonial fishing town of La Union on the Gulf of Fonseca.

Looking to bypass Honduras and go directly to Nicaragua, we paid a minimal fee to take passage on a 25-foot open boat. It was crossing the open water of the gulf to make its weekly delivery of groceries to the outer islands. The rising sun began to kiss the morning tides of the harbor as people and their gear made their way onto the boat. In the absence of a pier, the method of loading the cargo boat went like this: two men pushed a large, flat one-axle cart with car tires through the water. This pushcart carried groceries, building materials and passengers. Of course, this only worked until the tide rose above the height of the cart; after that, people were on their own to get their gear and themselves onto the boat. The ingenuity of their system was fascinating to watch. Latecomers had to put their children and goods on their shoulders and wade to the cargo boat. Along with people, this working skiff carried construction materials and weekly provisions to the folks who lived on the offshore islands.

After a late breakfast and people watching, the tide was too high for Leslie and me to ride the cart so we had to wade aboard. I removed my shirt and money belt and balanced my pack on my head. My polyester trousers and Teva sandals would dry quickly. Leslie, however, was wearing jeans and hiking boots. Her other pair of shoes were flip-flops, which wouldn't stay on her feet in the water. She had no choice but to wade in her boots and unfortunately spent the crossing wet. As I jockeyed for my favorite position on the bow, I watched Leslie help other passengers with their belongings. She chatted easily with the locals in her perfect Spanish and shared wet candy with everyone.

The sky was empty, but that didn't seem to make a difference to the seas. Five minutes away from our mooring, a heavy chop began smashing into the boat, rocking us up and down. The churning sea was slapping the side of our little 25-foot skiff and sending water over the edge, soaking everyone and everything within. The first mate covered the passengers with a large plastic tarp in an attempt to keep them dry while he bailed the accumulating water. Pinned in the very bow, I kept fairly dry and was loving the view. The young but seasoned captain skillfully steered through the next rising wall of water. The swells were large enough that everyone, passengers and crew alike, were afraid that our craft was going to capsize. We were all filled with a nervous tension, if not a sense of impending doom. This was made worse by the fact that there weren't any life preservers on board and we were several miles off the coast. The two-hour trip turned into a three-and-a-half-hour roller-coaster ride from hell, but thankfully we finally made it to the island.

We anchored about a hundred feet from the beach, and the passengers disembarked with their gear by rowboats and dugouts. Leslie asked the Spanish-speaking captain why there weren't any docks built along the shore, and he explained that the shifting sand in the open water and the huge waves make it impossible to set pilings. While the island inhabitants unloaded the groceries and other goods with rowboats, a few new commuters climbed into the skiff, oblivious to the chalk-white faces of the frightened passengers already on board. The young captain had a family to support, so despite the heavy seas, he would venture forth on the second leg of the trip.

Leslie and I were nervously discussing our options when we were told that the next boat wouldn't arrive until the following week. We were eager to be on our way to Nicaragua but didn't relish drowning in the process. While we were debating on whether to continue or not, a merchant was unloading his toys and candy. In a moment of inspiration, Leslie bartered for his only two plastic soccer balls and two inflatable globes. Emptying our daypacks, we put one of each inflatable inside them, thus inventing two flotation devices. Leslie felt reasonably confident with our new life preservers, so we made our survival plan in hushed voices even though no one spoke English. It was frightening to think that this was not a group of good swimmers. If we capsized, we agreed to drop our clothes and swim away from the boat as quickly as possible using our new floats. Once clear, we'd regroup and swim to shore.

Back out on the gulf, the turquoise water was still angry but not quite as turbulent. Once again I was on the bow and feeling more confident wearing the improvised life preserver. Everyone else was under the black tarp trying to avoid the bath we were still taking, but to me, the fresh air and breathtaking scenery were worth licking the saltwater off my face. The captain was masterfully navigating the big swells and the first mate was still bailing, but the danger from the first leg had subsided and we started making good time.

In the distance, I could make out the dramatic volcano on the coast with cloud after cloud dragging across its coned summit. The plentiful rainfall accounted for the extraordinarily fertile valleys, which an infinite number of horses grazed. If I were going to die, this would be the place to do it. Amongst these incredibly beautiful, rolling waves my spirit never felt more exhilarated. Volcan Cosquina, our destination, was looming large on the horizon, but it took another hour to arrive. I was elated to be on land again.

In Potosi, Leslie and I cleared customs in what looked like a chicken shed, then walked into town. We bought beer from the only store. Conversation in the store was difficult because of the constant hum of an engine. I was hoping it was a generator for refrigeration, but it turned out to be a tortilla-grinding machine. The townspeople brought last year's dried corn in buckets on their heads to the store, then the store owner added a little water to the corn and used his grinding machine to make perfect paste for tortillas. The store kept 10 percent of the corn brought in as its grinding fee.

Leslie and I were trying to hitch a ride to the next town in the late afternoon. A dust cloud down the road signaled the presence of a real honest-to-God cattle drive. Leslie and I were an audience of two as we watched the debonair cowboys, seated in old-fashioned wooden saddles, cracking whips and leading young, spirited horses and noisy cattle through the center of the village.

After the cattle train moved through and the dust cleared, Leslie chatted with some children playing nearby. They were shyly interested in our soccer balls and globes. She joked with the children, telling them these balls were important aquatic equipment until they realized she was teasing. I selfishly grabbed a globe, deflated it and put it in my pack. Leslie told the oldest child to give the other globe to his father. The children happily kicked the three balls down the unpaved street. The setting sun, the warm beer and the sound of happy children were very comforting. We were so content after a day that seemed to last a week.

That summer in Boston Leslie introduced me to a fellow traveler and friend Marco Werman. "So you're the wild hitchhiker I've heard so much about. I want to interview you on my NPR show *The World*." Wow! A week later, Marco thumbed through my seven swollen passports as we talked for an hour. I told his 2½ million listeners weird and wonderful stories of my 30 years of life on the road, about experiencing extraordinary kindness and the excitement of the unknown when you're camping and hitchhiking the world.

19
Little Lover

Since the days of the Vietnam War back in the '60s, Thailand has been the recreational center for sex, drugs and rock 'n' roll. Fifty years later, with tourists replacing soldiers, Thailand still indulged some of the more sublime tastes of yesteryear.

After a six-month journey through India and two months in Nepal, I stopped in Chiang Mai on my way back home. Chiang Mai is the northernmost tourist city of Thailand. I found a cheap room at a local guesthouse called the Lotus. It was appropriately named for the lovely scented flowers that seemed to grow everywhere in the region. The Lotus had a courtyard surrounded by tall, thick walls that offer relief from the busy street outside. At the center of the courtyard is a pretty, cascading fountain that soothingly drowns out all the noise of the city.

Taking my coffee into this luscious courtyard, I heard the owner making the same pitch he had given me an hour earlier to yet another tourist. "An hour elephant ride, an hour raft ride, lunch at a hill tribe village, finished by an hour hike through the jungle; all this for a major discounted price by staying at the Lotus." The reasonable rate of $5 a night and the $1 banana pancakes is the bargain; the tours being sold are not. If the owner can fill just half of his 12-seater van daily, he is making an extremely good living.

The innkeeper's latest target turned out to be a young woman dressed in Rajasthan hippie clothes, toting a small backpack and a groovy handbag. With long, thick black hair and perfect skin, at five-foot ten, she was probably the most striking woman I had ever seen. She took a room two doors down from mine, came back out to the courtyard and sat down. Kamala was a 24-year-old West Indian who had grown up in Toronto. She carried herself with confidence and candor, and it was evident she was a liberated solo traveler, reflecting her Canadian origins.

Kamala told me she had spent the last six months touring India. We discussed our different experiences and a shared love for the subcontinent. We were both in awe of the diversity of everything about it, from religion to culture. We talked about the contrast between the beauty and the filth of India's teeming humanity. I admired her full-lipped, dazzling smile as we laughed about the distinctive smells of India.

Kamala confided that she had spent the last month visiting relatives in the village where her parents were born. It turned out to be a bittersweet experience. She was welcomed as family and yet at the same time she was an outcast. An independent girl, Kamala felt like she had been held captive to the family kitchen and their compound. Having just been sprung from her apparently repressive extended family, Kamala was anxious to take advantage of northern Thailand in the 10 days she had before leaving for New Zealand. India's strict Hindu traditions regarding women didn't sit well with this wanderer.

She stole a wary glance at the bustling street. The mini-buses swarmed with clean tourists, sporting fresh beach tans, who were off to their next day's tour. "The hamster wheel of tourism," she remarked with a sigh. I laughed and enticed her with my plan. "Tomorrow the place I am heading to is three hours northeast of here on the Burmese border. It's in the region of Mae Hong Son where there are isolated hill tribes in unspoiled nature. With the Me Pai River meandering slowly through, it's literally where the jungle meets the mountains." Kamala was eager to join me on this journey. She understood that wandering isn't about getting to a destination; it's about the spontaneous discoveries that happen along the way. To really experience travel as an adventurer, you have to be willing to take the leap of faith that you will not only survive getting off the tour bus but will thrive because of it.

The following morning Kamala and I met up and hitched pickup trucks to Tha Pong Daeng. We boarded a longtail, which is a flat-bottom boat made of teak. A car engine suspended off the back of the boat with a 12-foot-long propeller shaft makes it a perfect waterbus for shallow rivers. We rode with at least 20 locals and their groceries and luggage going from village to village on the wide, shallow Me Pai River.

One tiny village looked inviting, so Kamala and I decided to disembark. Everything in this village appeared to be made of bamboo: boats, fences, ox carts, furniture, even the houses. The stilt homes were made exclusively from split bamboo pinned together with woven teak leaves for the roofs. Not a metal nail in the entire structure.

Making friends with a local tradesman, Kamala was offered one of the beautiful bamboo cottages for the night, and I set my tent up by the river. We got up early the next morning and helped the bamboo cutter stack, tie and role his bundles to the river. Once these bamboo bundles hit the water, they are as buoyant as a boat and a little roly-poly. The bamboo-cutter was taking his wares downstream to sell. He tied three bamboo parcels together as a raft and invited us to join him on the journey. As the raft meandered the four hours down the river, we all took turns using a pole to keep it in the current. It was a hot day, so Kamala and I swam and frolicked in the murky mountain water. Though no roads could be seen, an occasional farmhouse dotted the banks in the abundance of jungle that surrounded us.

Drifting around a corner, we came upon another tiny village of loggers with elephants pulling logs to their sawmill. The fragrance of freshly cut lumber was beautiful. The dozen or so farmers were using the labors of the elephants to produce some of the most valuable and beautiful wood on the planet - teak. Kamala, a huge elephant enthusiast, was ready to 'jump off' again and suggested we go ashore. We grabbed our little pack wrapped in a garbage bag, thanked our bamboo buddy and waded ashore to the teak village.

We met some of the workers and communicated again through mime and dance that we wanted to put up our tent and camp by the beach. Using song and mime, I inquired about when the lumber truck they were loading was heading to town. They told us with big, easy smiles that in two days' time the truck would be leaving and we were welcome to climb aboard. I spent the rest of the afternoon checking out the teak operation, and Kamala spent most of it loving the elephants. She and what appeared to be the youngest elephant instantly fell in love. Kamala named the elephant her "Little Lover." It was an incredible experience to swim with Kamala's giant pet. Then, to my dismay, Kamala fed Little Lover all of our bananas. Luckily, later on the villagers offered us food. Not wanting to appear too needy, we politely declined the invitation, but the gracious Thai people insisted. After a lovely meal of fish and rice, the villagers headed for bed. Kamala and I wandered back down to the beach, where we found the elephants shackled for the night.

After three nights of maintaining a companionable distance, there was a crackling energy surging between us. With a half moon shining on the dappled river, Kamala was positively radiant. We watched the mesmerizing effects of the warm wind on the surface of the slow river and the distortions of the half-moon and Milky Way. She went over to Little Lover, who kneeled down to allow Kamala to walk up her trunk and onto her back. I tried to follow, but Little Lover stood up abruptly and pushed me away with her trunk. Kamala found this wildly funny and showed no signs of coming down. I grabbed the elephant's ear and Kamala's leg to gracelessly climb up. Both of us were now straddling the prickly back of this gently swaying creature. Watching the riotous stars, I began massaging Kamala's shoulders. Relaxing into my hands, I took her purring pleasure as the encouragement to add a more amorous intensity. My heart was in her care, and I kissed her. Kamala responded in kind, and we entered into the realm of pure pleasure. At first I couldn't tell if the extra appendage was Kamala's clumsy attempt at exploration. Then I realized this other presence was that of Little Lover's trunk poking, probing, sniffing and intertwining with our bodies. Balancing this beauty on the back of her jealous pet gave new meaning to a threesome!

After two glorious days of riverside hide-and-seek, we set off with the smiling, knowing teak farmers, curious as to where the lumber truck might lead us next. Driving up a dusty single-lane mountain path, we intersected a wider dirt road and took a clue from our driver that this would be a good spot to depart. It is important to stay on the main roads in this region because of the secret poppy fields. Under the radar of the Thai government, both the Thai and hill tribes cultivate the fields for the cash crop they yield. Indeed, the next Toyota truck we hitched was filled with farmers with the black sticky fingers of processing. One young man in broken English told us of a weekly market at a Hmong village further up in the mountains. Six hours, three trucks and a whole lot of walking later, we finally found the remote Chinese enclave tucked deep into the folds of these secluded mountains.

This nomadic clan had sought distance from their native country some 200 years ago. Without electricity and little influence from the rest of the world, these tenth-generation refugees forgot to evolve, as if that was their intention. The women of this particular tribe of the Blue Hmong were adorned with massive silver earrings, necklaces and bangles. Their pleated dresses and waistcoats were mostly shades of indigo and heavily embroidered with cross-stitch. Kamala and I were intrigued by the women's large hairdos, which were sculpted dramatically off the forehead into 10-inch-high beehives. Everything about the dress indicated the furthest reaches of society, except the plastic sandals we recognized from mainstream Thailand.

On a steep hillside we walked around arm in arm, observing the preparations for market. Although we saw a man butchering a pig, it was mostly women and children who were setting up table after table laden with food, tools, fabric, dyes, jewelry and sandals. We watched as a young boy of about 10 came swaggering down a steep mountain path riding on the back of a huge water buffalo. The smell of good things cooking for tomorrow's fair was wafting heavily in the air. Kamala used her inventive mime techniques to communicate with a friendly older woman and procured our next honeymoon suite: a dry shed with a fresh hay floor was a perfect

94

place to set up our tent. With the sun dropping dramatically behind the steep, terraced rice fields, we retreated for the warmth of each other's body inside our small shed.

Dawn brought the renewed sounds and smells of market day, which came to life with the robust activity of the villagers' children. Both the boys and the girls wore straight black bangs that framed their round faces. Boundless energy ran them around on fat little legs. These delightful, noisy children weren't afraid to show their curiosity as they crowded around us, smiling and laughing. We could never count them nor will we ever forget them.

Market day was a circus of colors, smells and characters, and we shopped and ate our way through it all. We passed a table of new and used tools: a worn-out hoe, a broken machete and the curious curved blades of the poppy knife, still sticky with opium. These people recycled everything! Another stall was selling traditional Hmong clothing. Kamala was drawn to a crazy pair of men's pants. They were perfectly patched in the butt and comfortably worn. She was intrigued by the groovy, hypnotic patterns of the cross-stitch. As Kamala held them next to her waist, sizing them up, the woman at the stall looked askance and pointed to me. I understood her distress and said, "Of course they are for me," and quickly pulled out some Thai Baht to pay for them. This *faux pas* of Kamala's was the equivalent of me holding up a women's brassiere to size it up for myself. I whispered in her ear as we left the stall with the pants, "Merry Christmas, darling."

Taking refuge once again in our tiny little shack, we rested and cleaned off the day's dust. The sound of music lured us out into the last of the sunset. We saw a crowd gathering around a huge fire and joined in on one of the many log seats. Two older, freshly scrubbed men, who were wearing the new version of pants I had bought Kamala earlier in the day, immediately installed themselves on either side of Kamala and me like a set of rustic bookends. The music came from a man next to the fire, playing an instrument I can best describe as a mouth organ. It was a large, wooden flute-like instrument with finger holes on top and five various-sized reeds coming out the bottom; the longest one reached his knee. The ancient notes it produced had an incredible range of highs and lows. If the sounds were eerie, then the accompanying dance was equally as mysterious. With the fire illuminating his movements, the dancer slowly lifted one leg as if climbing over an invisible log. In a theatrical spin, he turned his face toward the sky and then crouched down into a ball. Throughout this combination of acrobatics and "tai chi" ballet he never once broke the rhythm of music and movement. While we were entranced with this performer, the bookend brothers were constantly passing Kamala and me a jug of strong sake and a corncob pipe. After a dreamy hour of this, Kamala leaned over with a kiss and said, "Thank you for a wonderful week of sex, drugs and rock and roll." With a lazy lopsided smile I responded, "Northern Thai-style."

Little Lover, Thailand

20
Swinging a Hammer in the U.S.

Venezuela is an ecologically diverse country. It has Andean peaks, Caribbean coastline, Amazonian jungle, rolling savannahs, grasslands teeming with wildlife, and tabletop mountains. The Pemom Indians call the tabletop mountains Tepul; two billion years old, they are home to Angel Falls, the world's highest waterfall. At 3,000 feet, these falls are as high as a 300-story building and 16 times taller than Niagara.

There's a definite season to see Angel Falls. In the rainy season there's plenty of water in the river, but the view is often obscured by fog. Tucked close to the Guyanese border up the Rio la Paragua, the sleepy little town of Canaima is the launching pad for Angel Falls. I was lucky that it had rained the night before so the river was just deep enough for me to catch what was probably one of the last sightseeing boats of the season.

The long, narrow dugout had a big engine, and a strong local native in the front with a huge paddle directing us through the rocks and rapids. We went fast enough upstream so that when we hit shallow spots, the boat scraped right over them. "Low water, no problem, fast and furious," shouted the captain with a thick Spanish accent over the roar of the engine. An hour and a half into the trip, we got our first view of the falls. It was astonishing to see its infinitely cascading water. We scurried up the wet rocks and ate lunch, enjoying the sunshine and cooling effects of the mist from the tallest waterfalls on the planet.

Back at the camp, I was fortunate enough to share a long coffee break with three bush pilots. Rodrigo, one of the pilots, told me, "Venezuela is a weird place. There is so much oil money floating around that there's no need to promote tourism." I learned that the government subsidizes fuel to the point that some Venezuelans are obsessed with the giant, gas-guzzling American muscle cars of the '70s. If you ever wonder where your neighbor's jacked-up super V8 Camaro is now, it could be a taxi in Caracas. These souped-up classics are still racing each other, stoplight to stoplight, at six miles to the gallon.

One of the pilots mentioned that he thought that America was about "opportunity." During the course of our conversation, it became clear that these bush pilots didn't make that much money and were worried about crime in their neighborhoods. Every one of them was sure that the road to wealth and security was in America. When I argued that the cost of living in my hometown was so high that it was hard to save money, they responded by saying, "But it's safe." Who can argue with that? However, I pointed out that in the U.S., pilots start out making as much as bus drivers. Never mind that the U.S. has its own brand of poverty, crime and corruption.

After a two-hour chat, Rodrigo invited me to fly back with him to Ciudad Bolivar. The take-off was intense, with an abbreviated runway and a wall of jungle directly in front of us threatening to kiss the wheels of Rodrigo's Cessna. Showing off his aerial prowess, Rodrigo spiraled around vertical cliffs, showing me his favorite waterfalls. He shared with me the story of how Angel Falls got its name. In 1937, an American bush pilot named Jimmy Angel crashed his plane while attempting to land on a tabletop mountain in search of gold. Jimmy lived to tell the tale after being rescued by local tribesmen. Rodrigo roared uncomfortably close over the tabletops to show me where Jimmy had crashed his plane.

Rodrigo also told me about the erosion that formed tabletop mountains. The flora and fauna are unique to each of the tabletop mountains because they had all separated a billion years ago. The Canaima National Park is 3,000 square kilometers and boasts some of the highest waterfalls in the world. As a rock climber, I found these sheer cliffs nothing short of outrageous, especially viewed at close range from Rodrigo's tiny airplane. It was extraordinary to see

Angel Falls from this vantage point. It's hard to appreciate the grand scheme of God's world if it's viewed only from the ground. In the air, at low altitude, you see more details hidden in the shadows. As giddy as a schoolboy on a merry-go-round, I opened the window and tried to feel the overspray of these massive waterfalls. The sensation of turbulence from the falling water and the steep angulation of the plane were electrifying!

As our flight continued, it became clear that Rodrigo hadn't been entirely altruistic about inviting me on a free ride. He continually asked me how much he might earn in the States and was very interested in my dad's construction business, explaining that he had carpentry skills. Rodrigo confessed that he wanted to live in America and raise his family in safety. Finally, he blurted out, "Could you sponsor me to come to America?" Wow. This guy, who makes his living flying a bush plane around some of the most beautiful landscape in the world, would trade it all for swinging a hammer in the U.S. I was reminded yet again how much I take for granted my U.S. passport and the opportunity to make easy money!

Angel Falls, Venezuela

21

Going Through a Woman's Purse

In a place called Christiania, on a picturesque peninsula in Denmark, hippies had taken over an old abandoned military encampment. They staged a long-term love-in, and to this day Christiania remains an active commune. I had a great conversation with the bartender of one of its many legal outdoor "coffeehouses." We talked about how thirty years ago in 1969, the Summer of Love, LSD, birth control, and the waterbed changed not only the United States but also northern Europe. I laughed at his joke about the summer of 1969 inspiring the name for a sex position. We also discussed the term "hippie," middle-class kids exploring their many options, and that it may have come from the English word "hypocrite." We decided that the Vietnam War with its mandatory draft had a lot to do with that radical era.

Then the bartender asked me where I was from and where I was staying. I told him that my tent was set up by the pond. With a worried look he told me, "Don't trust any of these people. They come across all hippie-love, but most of them are just bullshit." I nervously returned to my tent. The flap was open, and there was a beautiful wide-eyed Spanish gypsy lying flat on her back on my sleeping pad. She was topless and stunning. She'd found my magic-marker for making hitchhiking signs and was just finishing up a large self-portrait on the ceiling of my domed tent. After a few minutes I realized that she was tripping her ass off on LSD and couldn't comprehend that this was my house, my stuff. She didn't seem to want to leave, so I forcibly grabbed my marker and her handbag and lured her out of the tent with it. Rifling through her handbag, I found my headlamp and leather journal. The bartender was right: crazy, drugged-up hippies can't be trusted. For the next six months I was reminded of the topless gypsy girl when I woke up every morning to her glowing face staring down at me. Thank God she was a good artist.

Lucy in the Sky with Diamonds, Denmark

22
Cerebral Malaria

I owe my life to Sarah and Scott, a young, wealthy couple from South Africa whose cocktail party I crashed in Zimbabwe. Their houseboat was the finish line for an international rowing regatta on the Zambezi River. The day before the race, I was swimming on the top of Victoria Falls and met up with some of the Oxford women's rowing team from the U.K. Oxford and Pretoria were among the universities competing in the international regatta the following day. But that afternoon the girls were hanging out with me on top of the falls. We were all stunned by the beautiful views of the Zambezi snaking far out into the countryside and the wild zebras drinking on the opposite bank.

One of the many impressive features of Victoria Falls is a natural rock chair called "The Devil's Throne." I was eavesdropping on a guide who was teaching another couple how the test of courage is to come over the crest of the waterfall and sit on the throne. With the water thrusting over your shoulders, you literally look down hundreds of feet between your legs into the depths of this massive waterfall. Having the nerve to contemplate and then execute this harrowing feat was something I took upon myself to encourage the girls of the Oxford rowing team to try. A few of these strong, young women had the guts to go for it.

My own nerves were put to the test the next day when I boarded an ostentatious floating home uninvited. I passed myself off as someone who belonged to this very English houseboat party with a jazz band on the upper deck and tuxedoed black waiters wearing white gloves passing out champagne and hors d'oeuvres. Also on the boat was a regatta official with a stopwatch. He was in charge of registering the winners as they crossed the finish line. The majority of partygoers on this vessel were in support of South Africa's hopeful Pretoria team.

I was drinking champagne and flirting with a lovely beauty named Sarah when a young man came over and interrupted. "How do you like my champagne, my houseboat and my girlfriend?" he asked in his South African accent. I turned beet red. He laughed as he slapped me on the back and introduced himself as Scott, and rather than throw me off his boat, he magnanimously invited me to enjoy the festivities. Scott's cocky nature revealed he held respect for another arrogant rooster rather than being threatened by a fraud. We bonded instantly.

The rowers were now coming down within view, and Scott fixed me with a stare and said, "You are at least rooting for our girls from Pretoria, aren't you, Kev?" "But of course," I said in my best Grey Poupon accent. Seconds later a shrill whistle blew to indicate the winning team was crossing the finish line. It turned out to be my waterfall friends from Oxford, and after shaking off the rigors of their well-won effort, one of them looked up and identified me on the stern. She gave me a big smile and wave, yelling, "Hi, Kevin!" I, in turn, smiled, waved and yelled my congratulations. The other Oxford women saw my familiar face and called out, making me conscious of all the attention. "I might've known you'd be playing with the girls on the other team," Scott quipped. A sheepish smile was my only reply.

A seasoned pilot, Scott had recently purchased a twin-engine plane and flew it solo all the way from California back to his home in South Africa. Wanting to show off his new aircraft, he invited me to come along while he flew potential investors from his farm in South Africa to a resort site in Mozambique. Since crashing his party Scott and I discovered we had tons in common and lots to talk about. In his early twenties Scott had spent time in the U.S. as a professional snow skier and was an avid nature buff. We shared a similar zeal for life's adventures. In spite of his wealth, he was unpretentious, friendly and charming to everyone he met, and his girlfriend Sarah was an incredible complement to his style.

We flew from Scott's farm near Kruger National Park in his six-seater, dual-propped turbo, with three middle-aged Chinese businessmen. A thousand feet in the air was the most astonishing vantage point from which to view the magnificent patchwork of whitewashed farms, orderly vineyards and herds of wild animals on the open plains of southern Africa. We crossed into Mozambique, where the landscape changed into miles and miles of coastal jungle and beach, undeveloped except for a few thatched-roof fishing huts.

Nearing the property which Scott was marketing, we could see twenty acres of cleared jungle with a grassy landing strip which made for a bumpy touchdown. A welcoming white beach on the edge of the Indian Ocean and the beginnings of a future restaurant greeted our arrival. A generator kept the beer cool so the potential investors could relax and imagine the possibilities. We walked the property with Scott's guests. The reticent Chinese played their cards extremely close to their chest, and it was difficult to gauge their level of interest. Nonetheless, Scott enthusiastically discussed the features and details. After the tour we climbed aboard the plane and headed back to Scott's farm.

After a lovely dinner later that night, I told Scott and Sarah more of my plans to travel the continent all the way up to Egypt. They were both delighted for my adventure, though Sarah cautioned me about the dangers of yellow fever and malaria, which were on the rise in Central Africa. The most serious type is cerebral malaria, though the French had recently developed an antidote. Sarah pressed me to purchase anti-malarial drugs before I went any further afield. Cerebral malaria is a mosquito-related illness, a parasite that blooms in the brain, causing pain, projectile vomiting, fever and, if left untreated, coma and death! While I listened to her, I was not optimistic about my chances of obtaining the pills. I knew they were expensive and very hard to come by in this part of the world. As the evening progressed and the wine flowed, Sarah became ever more insistent about my traveling with the drugs. Finally, despairing that I would move forward without locating a supply, she insisted that I accept the stash they kept in their plane's first-aid kit. In the face of her persistence and with some relief, I agreed.

Along with the pills came the instructions. Sarah shyly explained that in the event I showed any evidence of cerebral malaria I was not to swallow the first pill. Rather, I was to insert it rectally because of the tendency to vomit. The next pills could be taken orally if the first pill worked well enough to eliminate the vomiting. I packed the pills away in a safe place hoping never to need them.

Two and a half months after meeting Scott and Sarah, I was in the country of Burundi. Because of the extremely mountainous terrain, farming is challenging in this small land-locked country. The only surpluses for export are coffee and sugar. It is the tenth poorest country in the world due in part to civil wars, corruption and AIDS. Burundi's large population is disproportionate to the country's size, but its beautiful black people are colorful and friendly.

It was Christmas time and I was seeking out Gihingamuyaga, a Christian monastery that stands on the top of a remote hill in a pine-scented forest. After many miles of walking, I arrived at sunset and knocked on the massive oak monastery doors. I explained to the answering monk that I was a traveler looking for a place to pitch my tent and celebrate the holy holiday nearly upon us. Father David checked out my credentials and nodded his approval. He directed me to a room with its own toilet and sink and invited me to join in their dinner.

Once inside, I freshened up and set out to explore my new digs in the hour before dinner. Inside the monastery, African monks dressed in black hooded robes walked silently while going through their everyday duties. Thick stonewalls were embedded with religious mosaic tiles, and the oak molding, was heavily carved. Scented fragrances and picturesque gardens were what I might have expected in Europe, and I was delighted that this African monastery was equally as beautiful. The silence permeated everything and left me a little unnerved.

The distinctive tone of the dinner bell broke the silence and I followed my nose to the dining hall. Father Dave was beckoning me to join him and I eagerly and hungrily obliged. Over delicious home cooking I was happily engaged in conversation with this charming priest. We talked of many things, including his austere days as a youth beginning in Burundi and his later life in Rome. We laughed about his antics on his Vespa scooter negotiating the awful traffic in the city, and I laughed aloud as I gave him a generous slap on the back, calling him a 'wild man.' He and I chattered like a couple of blue jays when it suddenly occurred to me that we appeared to be the only ones talking. Is it this quiet all the day long, I wondered? I asked Father Dave, and he told me that ordinarily monks do take their meals in silence. "The silence helps to acquire tranquility of the soul and to maintain an endless dialogue with God," he explained.

I nearly fell out of my seat when one of the monks came up and reverently whispered to my new best friend Dave, addressing him as "bishop"! Apparently I had further breached religious etiquette by sitting to the right of the bishop during his meal, a spot reserved for the most high. Already singled out as being the only white guy in this holy place, I wasn't giving a favorable impression after being there for only an hour. Yikes! I lowered my tone and murmured some apologies for my boisterous behavior as Bishop Dave dismissed me from the table with a laugh and a huge smile.

Waking up in the modest but incredibly clean comforts of my room the day before Christmas should have found me safe, dry, happy and festive. However, that evening as I was standing at the toilet relieving myself while admiring my spotless room and the beautiful clean windows overlooking a rose courtyard, what I thought was a little gas turned out to be explosive diarrhea. By the time my bladder was empty, a sharp hot knife of pain stabbed my lower stomach, crippling me and bringing me to my knees. Holding the perfectly white western toilet, I projectile-vomited over the window, wall, toilet and sink. Projectile vomiting? Cerebral malaria!? Holy shit!

Panicked and thinking that I may well have contracted the cerebral malaria that Sarah had so vehemently warned me about, I knew it was imperative to act quickly with the remedy she had insisted on giving me. My condition was such that I barely had the will or energy to crawl back to my bed and rifle through my pack to find the pills. I ripped open the packaging, cleaned myself off with a shirt, and inserted the first pill as instructed, then focused desperately on keeping it there.

The pain in my lower stomach was so intense that I couldn't straighten my body. Fever turned into hallucinations and my head felt like it was going to explode. All I could think of was that I was going to die! I just moaned in my soiled bed, trying to keep that pill inside me. The next thing I remember was nuns cleaning my room and cooling me with wet sponges. Bishop Dave also looked in on me, and since it was Christmas Eve he was dressed in full purple regalia, which made for a dreamlike vision as he performed benedictions over me.

Later I learned that this parasite takes fourteen days to incubate and blooms into your brain and liver, poisoning your blood stream and causing massive damage. In two weeks, you can go from healthy to dead! After a week convalescing in the calm, gentle atmosphere of the monastery, both my body and spirit were restored and I was able to slowly resume my journey. I sent the empty packet of pills to Scott and Sarah with a note expressing my profound thanks. The treatment in my possession and my immediate response undoubtedly saved my life. But I was also grateful for the good words Dave the bishop sent up on my behalf. After all, God is in the details.

My African Angel, Burundi

23
A Goodwill Kilt

Being a rock climber gave me an edge up for getting church repaints, and in midsummer 2001 I was just finishing up another painting project that had me peering over the tops of the sugar maples in a classic New England hamlet. I was suspended in my harness on an old church spire enjoying the summer sun. My brother Michael pulled up to the church one afternoon and told me that Dad was planning a family reunion of sorts in Scotland. Since I didn't have a cell phone, Michael drove to New Hampshire to see if I was on board.

The McNallys have a strong strain of Scottish blood, and a trip to our homeland was something my dad had always wanted us to do. He and my oldest brother, EJ, had just finished a two-year project building a home in Florida for a wealthy Scotsman. This client fueled Dad's enthusiasm for the trip by suggesting an itinerary that promised an amazing visit. It was complete with castle accommodations of the highest caliber.

"Wow!" My wallet and I balked at the grand scale of such a visit until Mike told me that Dad was paying for most everything once we got there. I was relieved and excited but a bit concerned about not completing all my painting jobs before the end of the short New England summer. Still, I hadn't done all that much traveling with my family. Mike sensed that I was waffling and slyly sweetened the proposal by saying he and one of our brothers, Brian, would help me with airfare on one condition: I had to wear a kilt for one month starting immediately, Scottish style - no underwear. I was equal parts amused and appalled at my brothers' twisted sense of humor, knowing that I climb ladders for a living. I agreed and we shook on it.

Now kilts were hard to find, and the ones that I did find were terribly expensive. I set my mind on getting a reasonable facsimile that wouldn't crunch my meager budget. I first asked my niece Greta if she had any leftover uniforms from her Catholic school days. She said she had given hers to the Goodwill and suggested I go look there for a kilt. Sure enough, Goodwill had a whole rack of discarded schoolgirl kilts, and I found three for $10 that fit me and my budget. I saved the two kilts that were in the best condition for Scotland. I also purchased accessories such as a wide leather belt with an embossed buckle, a kilt pin and a man purse. I wore the rattiest kilt for finishing up the steeple paint job. I modified the skirt by using the kilt pin to close the pleats between my legs to create shorts for discretion. I wore a swami belt that went around my waist so the extra pleats didn't bunch up at my crotch, and in this breezy manner I finished the last week of steeple painting to the many astonished looks of the locals.

The journey towards Scotland started in Boston, traveling standby in full Scottish regalia. I chose the green-and-black woven wool tartan and accessorized with a black sweater over a crisp white shirt. My black cross-country skiing knee socks were fit into a pair of expensive black leather shoes, and completing the effect was a man purse displayed proudly on my right hip. The entire ensemble was designed by Goodwill.

When you travel standby, there is a dress code standard, and when I left Boston, the Irish American ticket agent remarked how regal I looked. The final leg of air travel was out of New York's JFK, and I arrived Tuesday hoping to get on an evening flight. Sashaying up to the ticket counter, I was assisted by the next agent, a black middle-aged New York woman who gave me a very unfriendly once-over. The sneer on her face told me she was not enchanted with my appearance and she confirmed my suspicions when she said, "Well, what have we here, a cross-dresser on a standby ticket?" I gave her my most engaging smile and tried to soften her with the details of my family reunion in Scotland. I corrected her that I was not sporting a skirt but a kilt. Big mistake! She told me that I would not be boarding the plane in the costume in which I was attired. I retreated to my seat figuring tomorrow night would prove more fruitful for getting a flight.

I always enjoy people watching in an airport, especially at the frenzied pace in JFK. The stares that came my way were fun to read. People either gave me high appraisals or thought I was a freak, much like the differing reactions of the ticket agents. The following evening I waited to see what would unfold with the next ticket agent. To my total dismay, the same ticket agent of the night before had resumed her place as sentry. With my Scottish posturing wilting somewhat, I trudged up to her desk again and reluctantly asked about standby availability. On tiptoes she peered over her specs, took me in all the way down to my black wingtips and said absolutely nothing as she wrote down my name and said, "Next." Now my pleats were really starting to itch as I sat down heavily in my chair and contemplated the situation. I knew that changing clothes might greatly increase my odds of flying that night even if it meant losing the bet to my brothers. I watched as the others on standby were called; at last I heard my name. I jumped up and ran over to the fashion police agent with a flicker of hope. With no warmth in her voice or demeanor, she handed me my boarding pass and said, "You might be less of an embarrassment in first class. Now get to the gate. You're holding up the flight." I was rendered speechless and bolted for the plane.

After boarding the plane I relaxed into the large, cushy leather seats in first class on the eight-hour flight bound for Shannon, Ireland. The pretty flight attendant spoiled me with extra food and drink that I gobbled up the whole way over the ocean. I arrived in Ireland, a little jet-lagged and a little hung over and was surprised to find that the Irish were also a little hostile towards my uniform. With sneers and catcalls demeaning my manhood, I started my hitch across this country with a bit more trepidation. On the outskirts of Shannon, I perched my pack on a medium-sized boulder and hid behind it with my thumb out. I was finally picked up and enjoyed the midland's scenic rolling green hills while traveling with many Irish folks for three days. Tiny, white cottages dotted the landscape, as did the endless mossy stonewalls that bordered the narrow, winding roads.

Arriving in Dublin, I caught a boat across the Irish Sea to reach Holyhead. After crossing into the tiny country of Wales and still getting the stink-eye from the locals, I spilled over into England's Lake District, still riding my thumb north. With hauntingly beautiful lakes peppering the low hills, knolls and bumpy terrain, it was easy to see why this region was a popular tourist attraction. The weather here was tricky. It was sunny, windy and rainy, and the moody seasonal patterns presented a challenge for a cross-dresser crisscrossing the countryside. Although my pleats were billowing out in a Marilyn Monroe fashion making it more difficult to procure my next ride, it was a welcome relief from the damp wool that was chafing my ass.

I finally crossed over into Scotland's open moorland, which was blanketed by wide bracken and heather. In this southern region off the beaten path, I saw plenty of sheep, but I was looking around for the elusive brethren of kilts. Since I was heading north towards Edinburgh, the Scots knew a tourist when they saw one and finally rides came much easier. The last such ride was an old Scottish guy who pulled over in a beat-up, faded red Holden sedan. He had a huge craggy nose and bushy eyebrows that ran right into his ears. He looked every bit the proper Scottish gent in his tweed jacket and jaunty cap. He smoked a pipe that filled the cab with sweet tobacco. I asked what he hauled on his trailer hitch, and he told me that once a month he traveled to market with a single sheep from his farm, sold it at the auction, and returned with a younger sheep he'd purchased. He and the missus were trying to hang onto the farm since the kids had moved on. This kind soul never once mentioned my kilt and drove an extra 20 minutes out of his way to take me to my destination. He deposited me at Hanging Square at the base of the Royal Mile. There was festivity in the air with jugglers, puppeteers and loud bagpipers, and it was here, thank God, that I finally found people wearing kilts!

I made my way to Mulligan's, the appointed meeting place to catch up with my own clan. There they all were: Uncle Joe, Uncle Chick and Aunt Carolyn, my brothers Michael and Brian and my dear dad, Gene. Mulligan's was a lively, historic bar and the inn above it was where we were staying for the Edinburgh Festival, one of the biggest outdoor celebrations in the world. The "Fringe" activities of this event consist of over 2,000 stage productions across 250 venues. The highlight of this festival is the "Tattoo." Every night at the castle, troops of pipes and drums from around the world come to perform. International military regiments and even African tribes have played at the Tattoo over the years. The music on the colorful street was very festive!

Reunited with my family in this party-like atmosphere, I was at the butt end of good-natured jokes and rowdy jesting about my clothing. Michael and Brian were impressed that I had held up my end of the bargain. They had come to Edinburgh through Iceland and wanted to know about my overland route through Ireland. Since they were a few pints ahead of me, I detoured them with "It's a long story," as though that might explain everything. Bellying up to the bar and catching up to the spirit of things, I felt the unmistakable intrusion of a hand sliding its way up my backside. I turned around to see a pretty face framed in brilliant red hair. Whiskey breath infused her Scottish lilt, as she said, "Aye lad, I knew you for a true Scot the moment I laid eyes on ye." With a squeeze and a laugh she melted back into the crowd.

My clan had befriended Keenan, Mulligan's bouncer that night. A big military man with blue eyes that bored into everything like a challenge, he strode over and took in this new addition to the McNally tribe. Keenan was also wearing a kilt, but in contrast to the one I had, his tailored tartan kilt was full-blown military perfection, including the leather man purse with three tassels displayed prominently in front. After introductions were made, Keenan started in with my assassination. "Nice kilt, did you think it was ladies' night?" In Edinburgh, I didn't think I'd be subjected to the ridicule that I had endured for the past month. Both the kilt and Keenan were becoming a source of irritation. "Keenan, what the hell is wrong with my kilt?" I asked him. Keenan let out a belly laugh and said in his thick Scottish brogue to the delight of my clan, "That's not a man kilt, lad. It's a fuckin' school girl uniform!" Beat red, I howled, "Busted!" through the roar of their laughter.

24
Bury My Rolex?

While camping on the beach in Mexico's Yucatan Peninsula, I met a young traveler named Tom who, like me, also has a great deal of faith in life. He had just come from Guatemala where he'd spent two years in the Peace Corps. Prior to that, Tom had earned a history degree in Central American politics from Harvard. He was adventuresome, fluent in Spanish and eager to share the history of the region with me. "Written history is not necessarily what happened," Tom said. "It is what the winners have written down. More often than not, what we know and accept as history was created by authors with political agendas."

In the 1980s, in the middle of Guatemala's civil war, I spent enough time there to witness governmental manipulation, atrocity, genocide and the distortion of the facts by both the local and the foreign press. Tom told me that in many cases the events described in the newspapers or on television seem to have little bearing on what actually happened. The truth is lost except to those who witnessed it. They are the ones who bury the dead, pray for peace and do their best to keep going. They also preserve history in a personal way through the retelling of their stories to family and community.

Distortion of political events is not unique to Guatemala; it is also true of Palestine, Afghanistan, Iraq, Pakistan and Syria, to name a few. If the media, with its instantaneous technology, doesn't have to get it right today, imagine how many misrepresentations there are in history books. What about Constantine's 326 AD edition of the New Testament? Written history is created by extremely wealthy

---

and powerful men advancing their own causes. The federal reserve is not federal! Our government spends about two billion dollars a day on our military complex. Tom and I thought bailouts and subsidies to the rich were criminal. There seems to be very little difference between Democrats and Republicans, and voters have very little say in the direction of our military complex! People are inherently good while politics can be so bad. Tom and I both thought that the world would be a better place if the United Nations were run by Dutch mothers!

Being a scholar, Tom was a quick study and he learned a lot about bohemian travel in the two weeks we were together. He loved the freedom of hitchhiking and camping and mingled easily with the many people we encountered. The way we traveled allowed our lives to be shaped by circumstance. Tom's older brother was due to arrive for a visit the following week, and Tom wanted to impress him. He asked my advice about how to make an impact on his older brother. "Let's take him on a big adventure," I said.

Tom picked up his brother at the Cancun airport, and they took a taxi to the Hilton. If Tom could persuade this big-city lawyer into six days of adventure, they would meet me at the bus station the next day at noon. The next day they were there, and Tom introduced me to John. Initially, he appeared to be pretty uptight about this version of a vacation, but John trusted his brother enough to let Tom lead the way. Tom put John's wallet, gold chain and Rolex in a ziplock plastic bag; "Jesus, you're going to bury my Rolex?" spluttered John. "Yep," Tom said as he trotted across the street and discreetly buried it on the beach. Then he talked his older brother into giving away his suitcase and most of his clothing to a young couple. After John reloaded what remained into a used daypack, we took the bus to the outskirts of town and stopped at the first speed bump to hitch a ride on the back of a truck. We were on our way! As apprehensive as John might have been, Tom could barely contain his excitement.

Tom was the lead man on this trek, and since he and I had just visited this region a week ago, I said very little and let him be the guide. The first night we camped on the beach. We had two tents between the three of us. I slept in one with the gear, and John and Tom shared the other one. I overheard Tom telling his brother, "The beauty of getting lost is the adventure you have before you're found."

Turquoise waters, rugged cliffs and cold morning air gave way to a glorious sunrise, and at low tide we were able to sneak in the back way to visit the Mayan ruins of Tulum. Later that afternoon Tom used native lingo to strike up a conversation with a local fisherman. He had learned how to sing for our supper. "How much is the fish? Oh, good price! How much is it cooked? Okay, six o'clock is good. Can I bring Cokes for your children?" Tom, with his amiable attitude, possessed the ability to navigate different situations with ease and confidence. John, with his background in law, instinctively distrusted people. He observed his younger brother moving with the people and dancing through the circumstances.

Meandering through the jungle mountains of Chiapas, we got around by hitchhiking in open trucks and riding the roofs of chicken buses. It was so rejuvenating in this mountainous region. The lush tropical rainforest sustains an incredible variety of colorful birds, including toucans, parrots and the occasional macaw. The landscape also hosts cascading streams creating pristine swimming holes. Suspended cloud forests of primordial greens make it challenging to avoid low tree branches while riding on the top of tall 10-wheeler cargo trucks. The most memorable images are those of the friendly Mayans. These colorful people working their farms of banana, corn and coffee always stopped to look up, smile and wave as we drove by.

I could tell a great bond was forming between Tom and John as John let the wind and the sun of the open trucks blow his big-city suspicions away. In this breezy manner we traveled. We ate at markets and every other night found a cheap hotel. Tom went from scholarly student to patient, practiced teacher.

Upon our return, John retrieved his valuables right where Tom had buried them six days earlier. In parting ways, John shook my hand and thanked me for joining in his big adventure. "I have a new respect for the third world and it was well worth the minor inconveniences," he added with a smile. The brothers jumped in a cab headed for the airport.

Not only did John get a glimpse of his younger brother's bohemian lifestyle, he could now appreciate that the events of people's lives are not always accurately portrayed. I was impressed with John; he took a leap of faith to embrace unconventional adventure. John and Tom would now preserve history in a personal way by retelling their stories to family and friends for years to come.

"It's hard to bomb a country you've been to."
- Jimmy Carter

25
Dragon Dancers

I first met Suzanne in Guatemala. At the time my brothers Chris and Mike were traveling with me, and we were planning to make our weekly climb up Pacaya Volcano. My brothers and I were obsessed with this volcano and spent at least one night a week on it. Suzanne was packing her bags across the hall in the same cheap hotel when I invited her to join us.

It took us a few hours to hitch to the base of Pacaya and we began climbing at noon. To reach the top safely, you must get close to the summit no later than sunset. Most of the hike is on a straightforward trail, but near the end it becomes loose black volcanic ash and for every three steps up the steep slope, you slide back two. Loose ash mixed with broken black volcanic glass shreds a good pair of shoes, and our extra outer layer of clothing, worn just for the occasion, got trashed. We even put socks over our hands so we could scramble up the last brutally exhausting mile on all fours.

That night the wind blew towards us, and the taste of sulfur in the air came early. Pacaya Volcano is very active. It erupts often and aggressively and its conditions can change from week to week. It's important to approach this dragon at night so that you can see the edges of the safety zone. Only in the dark can you see the red lava balls that shoot hundreds of feet into the air. While the safety zone is fairly easy to read, one is dealing with a living geological entity and it is important to be alert in case the predictable becomes unpredictable.

My brothers and I loved to take other travelers up the volcano. The summit is 9,000 feet high. The heat from the volcano combined with other environmental factors means that the weather on the summit can be dramatically different than just a thousand feet below. The night we guided Suzanne up the mountain, the weather was clear and cold and the sky was filled with stars. The 30 mph wind was filled with volcanic ash, which sandblasted our skin.

Closing in on the summit, Chris shouted through the wind to Suzanne, "Keep your eye on the Dragon's mouth. No more headlamps. Stay close and if I tell you to run, run like hell!" To my surprise, Suzanne was still totally enthusiastic. Michael started restoring the three-foot-high lava rock wall from our previous camp, which served as protection from the unrelenting wind.

The Dragon was very much alive that night with a constantly changing rhythm. We timed the eruptions at roughly every three minutes. It sounds like an old man dying from smoking cigarettes; a wheeze turns into a cough and a cough into a rumble. The eruptions are so great that they can knock you to your knees!

From the edge of the opening of Pacaya, the 'game' is to have the courage to go to the edge of the broken cone and look into the Dragon's mouth between belches. Some newcomers will possibly take a peek into the Dragon's mouth and bid a hasty retreat, and for good reason; the molten inferno is extremely intense. Even from 200 feet above, the brightness of the bubbling lava pond in the volcano is blinding and the molten rock ebbs and flows dramatically. When you hear the volcano building up to spew molten magma and the ground starts shaking, you must run like hell back to the protection of the wall. From within, bright orange lava balls, half the size of garbage cans, shoot hundreds of feet in the air and flatten like pancakes when they land. Dragon dancers, such as my brothers, Suzanne and I, tempt fate by waiting a little longer and risk getting bit by the Dragon and its fiery fury. Back behind the safety of the wall in a sleeping bag, the side of your body touching the ground is burning up while the other side is freezing. We attempted to sleep but in reality, it's next to impossible.

The next day, on our way out, having taunted the Dragon, we laughed like warriors returning from combat. We compared the battle wounds of our accumulated cuts, burns, scrapes and torn clothing. Most amazing was the amount of black soot in our hair, ears and shoes. On the trail we passed a couple going up for the first time and they looked at our blackened, happy faces and nervously asked, "Is it dangerous? Is it worth it?" Suzanne, in her beautiful English accent, explained, "Summit before dark and find the black wall. That's your safety zone. Last night it erupted about every three minutes. That gives you enough time to look into the Dragon's mouth. As for 'Is it worth it?' It's the most exciting adventure Central America has to offer!" I knew right then and there I should continue traveling with this woman.

Pacaya Volcano, Guatemala

26
On the Road with Suzanne

Since our meeting in Guatemala, Suzanne had written me three letters in three months. One warm midsummer morning on a whim, I packed my bags and hitched to the airport. I spontaneously used a buddy pass to fly over the Atlantic to London. In the rain, armed only with a smile and flowers, I nervously waited for Suzanne on her stoop. Luckily, it turned out to be an amazing surprise! That night while she was cooking dinner I discreetly checked out Suzanne's closet. I can tell a lot about a person by the shoes they wear; where they've been and where they want to go by what has been worn and what is waiting to be worn. Suzanne's shoe collection confirmed that she was an ideal traveling partner. It was easy convincing her to take some time off to travel with me in Europe.

We spent a wonderful week in London and then began our travels by crossing the channel into France and hitching to the recently opened Czech Republic. Neither Suzanne nor I had ever seen a city like Prague. The people were high on their newly found freedom. Miraculously, Prague remained completely intact during World War II, escaping the devastation of many other European cities. Germany had not bombed it because Hitler planned to live in Prague after he won the war. Prague's ancient and attractive architecture sings to the soul.

Suzanne told me that the gypsies were scam artists in this region but I scarcely paid attention. While she was busy writing in her journal, I grabbed a big chunk of our money to exchange for the local currency and headed for the famous Karlovy Bridge. There I found a young dark-skinned man offering an extremely good rate of exchange. We went under the bridge, money changed hands and he quickly disappeared. I came up beaming like a rooster because I love black market deals. A merchant came over and asked me, "Did you just change money with that gypsy?" "No. Why?" I lied. "If you did, you just got ripped off," he confided. "That money he passes is fifteen-year-old Polish money." I confirmed it with one of his neighbors. They couldn't help but laugh as they calculated that the money I'd received in exchange for $200 US was worth about $1.80! Oops.

From Prague we were en route hitchhiking to Paris when a Dutch trucker heading for Marrakesh picked us up. The trucker's tales of Morocco with its historic glamour and budget accommodations convinced us that it would be a better destination than Paris. In less than five minutes Suzanne and I altered our plans and continued with him for the rest of the week.

Marrakesh is an old caravan town set in the foothills of the Atlas Mountains. Today the town square bustles with acrobats, dancers and musicians. Suzanne and I ate magnificently in one of the many open-air restaurants. Our accommodations were so romantic, with an amazing roof view, white linen on a massive feathery bed and warm breezes billowing the gauzy curtains. We relished all of this elegance at an incredibly affordable price.

Next, we headed to Chefchaouen, situated high up in the rugged Rif Mountains. This relaxed town is stunning. In its old part, there are narrow cobblestone streets and the wonderful Moroccan architecture has no hard lines, only soft curves; it flows like glacial blue water. The locals, attired in their long Muslim robes and leather slippers, openly enjoy their water pipes in the many cafes. In the clear mountain light of this ice-blue medieval town, Suzanne and I sipped sweet mint tea and enjoyed the relaxing mountain atmosphere. Suzanne picked up more key phrases in Arabic. Since she had lived all over the world and spent many years with her family in Muslim countries, Suzanne understood the cultural protocols and kept herself modestly covered.

One afternoon, the owner of our hotel suggested we visit an old, broken-down mosque not too far away. As we walked along, a half-dozen young teenage boys who were looking for trouble followed us and began tossing rocks in our direction. Since we were hiking uphill away from the boys, the rocks were falling short and posed no real threat. Suzanne pleaded with me to ignore their behavior, while she scolded them in their own language. Undeterred, they continued pelting rocks our way even as we entered the sanctuary of the mosque. While on the flat mosque roof, one large stone came too close for me to ignore and I instinctively retrieved it and threw it back at our antagonists on the ground below. Suzanne immediately realized I'd made a huge mistake. The hunt was on. These Muslim boys were hunters and now that I had responded, we were the hunted! We quickly left the mosque and retreated downhill but this put us at a tactical disadvantage. Zigzagging through the trees for protection, we ran for our lives the few miles back to our hotel!

That winter Suzanne and I traveled to India. We were among the few tourists in Kashmir, the disputed territory between Pakistan and India. There had been gun fighting on the street the year before, and most travelers were still leery of the region. We bargained with a local mountain guide to take us along the front range of the Himalayas. A cook and his pack pony accompanied the guide, Suzanne and me on this journey.

The scenery was breathtaking in the foothills of the tallest mountains in the world. We were enjoying a huge view on a rocky knoll. Our pony was grazing as the cook was making tea on a small fire. The atmosphere changed from completely relaxed to extremely tense when out of the west came two dark figures; even the pony seemed agitated. These were Pakistani border patrol. They were carrying large automatic weapons and came right up to us, thankfully saying the international Muslim greeting, "As-salamu alaykum" (peace be with you, my brothers) to which we replied, "Wa alaykumu s-salam" (and also to you, my brothers). They sat down for tea and in an attempt to look more peaceful, the two men wrapped their shawls around themselves to conceal their weapons so that only the rifle barrel resting on their neck was visible. They were gorgeous with their thick black hair flowing over their shoulders and heavy long black beards. Everything about them was black, down to their coal-black eyes. They never looked at or acknowledged Suzanne. They were Muslim warriors and gentlemen. I gave one of them a peace offering just to see him smile. It was my red Swiss army knife. When the men in black walked back toward the sunset and were out of sight, we nervously trotted east.

Late the next afternoon we came across an abandoned herder's shack to rest in for the night. We had an amazing meal and fire with a backdrop of the Himalayas at sunset. We were all getting ready for bed when the cook insisted on bringing the pony inside the tiny 10' x 12' shack. I refused to share our cramped sleeping quarters with a 1,000-pound, smelly, nervous beast who would step on me in the middle of the night, so I took the pony outside and tied him to the strongest of the two rotten columns holding up the porch. The four of us settled in for the night. Sometime in the early morning the pony got spooked and bolted, taking the rotten column he was tied to with him. With a huge crash the porch ceiling collapsed and swung into the building. It took a few minutes for Suzanne to find our flashlight and then to discover what had happened. The only window and door were completely blocked so we were trapped inside. It took an hour to kick a hole in the wall to get out of the shack and another three hours to find the pony in complete darkness. Our guide told me that a few years before the pony had witnessed its brother being killed by a leopard, which is why the cook had wanted to bring the pony into the cabin.

During my years of travel there have been many times when my ego ruled over my common sense. I traveled with Suzanne for two and a half years, and this 100-pound redhead from England continually enlightened me. When I charged in like a bull in a china shop, she invariably calmed the waters with her common sense and cultural awareness, making her a unique traveling mentor. She helped me understand my own struggle of ego verses spirit, and her sixth sense and sensitivity helped make global traveling safer, easier and ever more beautiful for me. Thanks, Suzanne! I miss you.

27

Little Beasts from Hell

In the early '80s I was camping for weeks by the famous mountain river Agua Azul in Chiapas, southern Mexico. There are countless limestone caves in this very steep rainforest terrain. Agua Azul (Blue Water) has thousands of natural pools that cascade from shell pool to shell pool to shell pool, making it one of the best swimming holes in the world. You can literally swim and dive for miles. Free camping downstream and swimming every day for many weeks was refreshing for both my budget and soul. However, it is also home to one of the worst little beasts from hell I have ever encountered. One regrettable day my companion Carlos and I woke to find hundreds of tiny ticks crawling all over us. I can live with spiders and snakes and I've learned to tolerate rats, but hundreds of ticks had me on the verge of hysteria!

Like all ticks, they went for the warm, moist, hidden spots of the body. We picked as many off as possible then hastily packed our infested gear and made a beeline into town for a decent hotel. We considered hiring a prostitute for the sole purpose of debugging the sensitive areas not visible in a mirror. I'm a bit fuzzy, but Carlos is downright hairy, and while I'm not particularly homophobic, exchanging services on one another took a lot of perseverance and alcohol. I now realize that I should have sprung for the prostitute rather than chancing the years of subsequent therapy!

Twenty years later in Newfoundland, a month into our hitchhiking trip, my nephew Will and I were overrun by black flies, tiny creatures with a ferocious bite. The cloud seemed to have darkened the sky, and they were biting the shit out of us. We were sucking them into our lungs and up our nose and going crazy. From a distance it looked like we were both having epileptic fits with our bodies twitching out of control and our arms flailing wildly. A leather-faced local stopped in her car, cracked the window and informed us with a laugh, that we were doing the "Newfoundland Wave." Her every word was punctuated by a cloud of exhaled cigarette smoke to ward off the little beasts. She told us the post offices on the island are required to sell mosquito jackets at this time of year, so we bolted to the nearest one. Fortunately, this inexpensive and essential jacket has a hood that completely covers the face and head. Thank you, Canada.

Three years later I used that very same mosquito jacket while hitchhiking south from Goose Bay, Labrador. I was dumped off by a young couple on their way to a remote fishing camp on the most isolated stretch of road in eastern Canada. I felt abandoned in spite of their promise to pick me up on their way back in three days' time. It was a hot sunny day in late spring when I noticed the sun was obscured by a rising, swirling cloud of mosquitoes. I was in the infamous Arctic wastelands, which is a breeding ground for mosquitoes that happens only two weeks a year.

I was about to have a harsh lesson in Arctic Terror. The first minutes of the attack were horrifying. Before I could get the mosquito jacket out of my pack, these winged tormentors descended on my face, eyes, ankles and hands. They were inside my nose, in my lungs and on every unclothed centimeter of my body. The couple of minutes it took to dig the jacket out sent me into a panic and a coughing fit. To be unprotected here, without a jacket or inside a tent, was suicide! These bloodsuckers have brought down caribou and moose. If I hadn't sought immediate protection, I could quite possibly have been dead by morning!

Blackened by these insects and bitten incessantly and painfully, I managed to put on my mosquito jacket and erect my tent. When I opened the tent to enter, part of the swarm followed me inside. In the zipped-up tent, I slapped, rolled and smashed the last of their bloody carcasses. Finally, I lay on my back exhausted and hyperventilating. Swollen and scratching, I didn't leave my tent for 24 hours, peeing in empty water bottles.

The next afternoon a light breeze came up and I ventured out of my safety zone for an extremely needed toilet break. They were still out there! Now I had hundreds of bites on my ass and upper thighs and I still needed to make a water run. And run it was! To make matters worse, at this time of year drinking from Arctic ponds and swamps is dangerous because of the billions of larvae in the stagnant water. I put a dirty sock over my water bottles and slowly filled them to prevent ingesting the larvae. All the while the hungry mosquitoes blackened my bare hands.

I continued to be literally trapped in my tent in the middle of nowhere. A few cars went by each day. When I heard them, I would quickly rush to unzip the tent and stand by the side of the road desperate for a ride. Would you pick up an unshaven barefoot guy in dirty long underwear with Kramer hair and swollen eyes, standing outside a tent thumbing in the middle of nowhere? I had spent three dismal days held hostage in the madness of the "Arctic Terror" before a lionhearted person stopped and waited for me to break camp. In all of nature, there is no predator as fierce or as frightening as the Arctic mosquito in Canada's tundra. There's just no outrunning them. Such is the pain of my recollection.

Arctic

28
The Great Wall

After days of hitchhiking in soaking weather I came down with a fever, headache and very sore throat. In Osaka, Japan I took the last dose of antibiotics, which I'd bought in an Indian pharmacy two years before. I figured this five-day broad-spectrum antibiotic would kill anything I had.

Saying goodbye to Japan, I boarded a ferry in Osaka and after a two-day passage would be in China. The year was 2003 and the SARS epidemic had begun spreading throughout Asia. There was a rumor that the Chinese were imposing quarantines on any ill passengers attempting to disembark from the boat. My fever was raging as I waited in line for the gangplank to lower to enter China. As we exited, Chinese authorities were scanning the crowd with a heat gun and pulling people aside. I put the ice from my drink into my mouth and hoped for the best, and to my relief, I passed customs and crossed into the pulsating streets of Shanghai.

Fast paced and polluted, Shanghai was a fascinating eclectic mix of old and new architecture. The "don't fix it unless it's broken" attitude appealed to me and I poked around for a week, meandering through the backstreets of the working-class neighborhoods. Eventually I caught a bus and left for Beijing. Wide streets paved this cultured metropolis, but for all its shine and modern amenities, I found it lacking the charm and character of Shanghai.

I had four objectives while I was here; the first was to get a ticket for the Trans-Siberian Railway; second and third, to get a visa for Mongolia and for Russia; and finally, to get a bridge for my missing molar.

A few months earlier, my dentist back in the States had informed me that there weren't any roots left beneath a bad molar, making a root canal pointless. He pulled the tooth that afternoon and told me to wait for the hole to heal, at which time he would fit a bridge for $2,800. I mumbled with my mouth full of bloody gauze that my car only cost $500!

So here I was in the nicest part of Beijing with all the embassies and European cafes. Fast food, fast paced, technically advanced and catering to the legions of tourists, this city had changed so much since I'd visited it 15 years ago. No longer did people wear the green-and-blue Mao uniforms and have only one bicycle per family. The Chinese were loving their new world of consumption. One bicycle per family was replaced by a drove of small, loud, smoky motorcycles, and the rich were now driving cars. The quiet, clean city was now choked with pollution and had a parking problem.

Dutch embassies are by far the most accommodating to anyone holding first world credentials, and since I didn't speak the local language, I headed there to inquire about a good dentist. After showing my passport and having my backpack x-rayed I was ushered into the empty waiting room at the Dutch embassy. I walked up to the brunette supermodel secretary sitting behind her glass desk. I couldn't help but stare; she was wearing the shortest of miniskirts. The words came slow as I finally asked to see the Consulate General. She scheduled me for the first available appointment the following month. I smiled and accepted the Consulate's business card as I said to this polished secretary, "You have a beautiful smile. Is there an embassy dentist you can recommend?" "Dr. Chow is the best in town," she told me and wrote his name and address on the back of the card.

The office was easy to find in the upmarket area of the city. Dr. Chow's office took up the whole fourth floor. The number four is very bad luck for the Chinese, much worse than our number thirteen. Evidently Dr. Chow wasn't too concerned about Chinese superstitions. I found a seat in the elegant waiting room of black leather, chrome and glass and struck up a conversation with a gentleman that turned out to be the ambassador of Kazakhstan. His abscessed tooth made him mumble and the smell of his rotten breath put a little physical distance in our amazing conversation, but I found him interesting as our discussion ranged from the cold war to the change in China. An hour and a half later, he was called in to the dentist.

Flashing the consulate business card for the third time, I reminded the receptionist that I needed to see Dr. Chow before the end of the day. Hours later, Dr. Chow, a small man with big glasses, introduced himself and I told him my dilemma: "I need a bridge. I have very little money and I am leaving on the train in ten days. By the way, did I mention that I'm a dear friend of the Consulate General of Holland?" I implored with as much sincerity as I could muster. With an exasperated sigh he quoted me $1,000 for gold and $600 for enamel. I asked him if he would do it for $450, seeing I was a dear friend of the Consulate General. Sighing again, he said $500 and promptly introduced me to a Dr. Lee, who took x-rays and impressions, then scheduled me to return in five days.

While waiting the five days for my next dental appointment I went to the Mongolian and Russian embassies, then signed up for a day tour of the Great Wall of China. Early the next morning the driver and the tour guide eyed me suspiciously as I clambered into their minivan with my enormous backpack. When our tour arrived at the Great Wall I told them I would see them in a couple of days for my free ride back. They rolled their eyes and had a conversation I didn't understand. I collected my gear and parted company with the group as I had intended to do all along. I lit out on my own away from the masses by heading in the opposite direction. I had tent, food and water assuring me comfort for "my tour" of China's Great Wall.

Twenty feet wide and just as high, this was more like a giant stone road than a wall. It held me in awe of how determined the Chinese were to deter their neighboring Mongolian raiders. The Ming Dynasty of China worked on the Great Wall for a hundred years but the Manchu Army stormed the Middle Kingdom and ruled China for the next two and a half centuries. Stout warriors with animated moustaches and dark features, these Mongolians were among the most notorious barbarians in history. Being superb horsemen, the fast and fierce Manchu Army pillaged, burned and raped their way through Eurasia, leaving raging floods of destruction in their wake. The Mongolian invader Genghis Khan said, "The strength of this wall depends on the courage of those who defend it." I was enraptured with man's creation.

On the second day I came to the end of the rebuilt section and climbed onto what was now a broken, crumbling path. That night I camped with fellow squatters in an old guard tower. These inhabitants were definitely not selling Coca Colas or postcards and they clearly thought I had taken a wrong turn somewhere. They were infatuated with my self-inflating sleep pad and headlamp. A few of these forgotten old folks were still dressed in decades-old Mao uniforms.

Centuries earlier, the Chinese used these towers as a beacon system. Frozen wolf carcasses, dung and wood provided the smoke signals to the next tower. Inside, the guard room was no larger than the area you could swing a cat in, and tonight the tiny twig of a fire was much more discreet and, unfortunately for these hungry squatters, didn't include any small dead animals. The flames cast a spooky glare on the homeless faces, which looked as old and cragged as the stonewalls of this forgotten place. Due to a lack of protein these old folks were at least a foot shorter than the present generation. This was the China I had come back to see.

When I returned four days later, my eyes were red and my whiskers wanted a shave. Thankfully I found the same guide and with a look on his face that could have curdled milk, he took in my smoky, smelly appearance. With barely enough tolerance and another eye roll, he allowed me to sit on my pack in the aisle. The driver was clearly disturbed that he had a dirty passenger who was riding without a seatbelt in his new Toyota van. In 15 years Beijing had gone from bicycles to brand-new tourist minivans that had seatbelt regulations. I barely recognized this China.

Back in the waiting room on the posh fourth floor of Dr. Chow's chrome office, I spent a lot of time cultivating new friendships. I arrived hours early for my appointment just to hobnob with the upper crust of European ex-pats. I met a beautiful fashion magazine editor, a secretary from the German embassy and an

Austrian tennis coach, to mention a few. True to his word, Dr. Lee with his French accent gave me a beautiful new bridge for $500.

I then purchased a ticket on the Trans-Siberian Railway for the journey to Russia. The ticket included sleeper car accommodations and very basic meals through China, Mongolia and seven of the nine time zones of Russia. This all-inclusive seven-day train trip was only $217!

From my seat on the train I could see the section of the Great Wall that I had just visited. The next afternoon the train passed yet another section of the ancient remnants of the Wall before finally veering off towards the Mongolian border. The Wall dramatically stretches out five and a half thousand miles like a dragon's tail. This man-made structure is so colossal it can be seen from the moon! The sheer force of effort to erect a project of this magnitude defies imagination.

A few mornings later I looked out the window onto the treeless high-plains desert of Mongolia and saw 20 horses lined up with a rope cobbling their front legs together while they were milked. Behind the milkmaid was her family shelter, a grey dome-like structure made of felted wool called a *yurt*. Surrounding the portable shelter was a small flock of sheep. Such is the nomadic life of many Mongolians.

On the Russian/Mongolian border the train was required to stop so that the mechanics could switch out the undercarriages to adapt to the Russian track width. The train cars were pulled into a huge warehouse. In the middle of the night the Russian border patrol tried in vain to empty the sleepy passengers from their cars, but a few of us stayed on board. It was fascinating to watch the transition. Hurricane lanterns cast a magical yellow glow on the dozens of men in old greasy overalls scurrying around the cars, wrenching off huge nuts the size of a man's head and sledge-hammering bolts out the size of a man's leg. The shed crane picked up our freed car and placed it onto a new Russian undercarriage. The entire process took all night. We were at the very beginnings of the nine-time-zone Russian train system.

29
The Lost Boys

I have often wondered about my good fortune to have been born in the United States with its opportunity, wealth and status. From war-torn, famine-stricken Africa, a young refugee from Sudan with great language skills welcomed me as I got off a bus in Kenya. His body had been crushed by the war, but his twisted smile and sparkling eyes spoke of the expansiveness of his spirit. After talking to him I came to realize that he made his meager living as a street hustler. "I escaped a war and you have come to visit me. Can I take you to my favorite inexpensive garden hotel?" I told him, "Sure, why not." After settling me into the hotel my new friend received a scant commission from the owner. Afterwards, this poor, intellectual man spent a quarter of his day's wages buying us coffee at the market and then proceeded to share his story. He began by telling me, "Brother, we are both so incredibly lucky today."

He was one of the "lost boys," a term given to the young men that fled Sudan. Along with two dozen other young men he made an epic journey traveling from his former home in the Darfur region of Sudan to seek refuge in Ethiopia. He told me that they had traveled hundreds of miles, fending off the murderous raiders and hungry lions that hunted them at night. The boys walked south using the stars for guidance and kept off the main trails because of landmines. He told me the most frightening part of the journey was to be at the end of the line, which the boys took turns at, as they quickly covered ground at night; two of his friends in the back of the line were taken by lions, and three others were shot by raiders. "But it all led to this perfect moment," he told me. Throughout my wanderings I've learned it is not money that makes life worthwhile, but the love in a person's heart and the optimism of a brand-new day.

30
Hanging with Elvis

When you travel, camp and hitchhike as much as I do, it is a statistical certainty that eventually you will be confronted by violence. Adapting to the wild side of life, I have developed a sixth sense of where danger might be and how to avoid it. Instinctively you might think that danger comes from slums or war-torn environments and therefore you may let your guard down when in small towns. It was on a small Indian reservation in the middle of Manitoba, Canada that I was witness to one of the most lawless places I have ever encountered.

On my fifth time around the world I began hitchhiking in Newfoundland, trying to cross Canada. Ontario is a wide, urban province, chock full of rich city dwellers and it kicked my ass. One stressed-out young fellow in a brand-new truck hollered out the window "Take the bus!" as he sped on past.

So I thought I was in the chilled-out heartland of Canada when I eventually crossed over to the farmland of Manitoba. Elvis was the name of the Nova Scotian who finally picked me up. He seemed normal enough. His classic baby-blue Buick was slightly tilted from the undersized spare tire on the front right. As Elvis kicked it up to 70 mph on the highway, we struck up a friendly conversation. When I asked him about the tire, he seemed reluctant to talk about it. I commented on his name, and he told me his mother was a huge fan of "The King." As the miles passed, Elvis said he was headed west to Medicine Hat for work. I was tired and sunburned, so I was happy to have a ride for the next couple of days. Elvis then confided he had a gas card but no money for food. I happily shared my peanut butter and jelly sandwiches with him as he drove us across the flat grain fields of Manitoba.

I was appreciative of the ride, but my suspicions about Elvis' agenda began creeping in when we stopped at a gas station. When other customers at this station came in to pay for their gas, Elvis charismatically inquired if he could fill up their tank with his gas card in exchange for the cash they were going to pay at the register. He offered a couple of extra dollars' worth of gas for the exchange. Some patrons politely declined, but Elvis was not deterred. He waited until a cash-paying customer would strike a deal. Meanwhile I was trying to keep busy checking his oil, washing the windows and inspecting the very worn spare tire on the front. I asked Elvis if he was going to use the cash he had made to replace the eroding tire, which was now showing its steel belt. Elvis again shrugged off my concerns. He pulled back out onto the treeless stretch of highway heading west and kicked it back up to 70. I just buckled up and tried not to think about it.

A few hours later Elvis exited off the highway. When I inquired as to the reason, he told me he had to visit a friend on the Cree reservation. My sixth sense slapped me on the side of the head. In hindsight I should have told Elvis to drop me off, but I figured a new ride would be hard to get so I kept quiet. The run-down wooden structures that dotted the dirty streets on the reservation registered as multi-family units of welfare. Elvis pulled up to a rough-looking stranger and asked, "Where's the good stuff?" My heart sank. This was the reason for the detour, and it turned out the friend Elvis was calling on was Mr. Crack Cocaine. I found myself wishing to be back on the side of the road waiting for a week rather than continuing with Elvis!

We zigged and zagged around the reservation until he stopped in front of a dilapidated shack of a house. Broken cars were strewn among dirty brown apartments with unwelcoming doors and broken windows. The barking dogs chained in the yards were another warning that made my hair stand on end. Elvis eagerly jumped out of the car and approached three guys who looked like they had escaped from a home for the bewildered. They were sitting outside in the weeds on a wet and rotting lime-green living room couch, passing a pipe. Elvis asked them, "Who's sellin' the good stuff?" He got the information he was seeking and with both feet pointing deeper into the slum, he turned to tell me he would return in 15 minutes. I made a desperate attempt to regain some control of events by pleading with Elvis to leave the car keys. With a short laugh he assured me once again, "Fifteen minutes" and walked away, eager to spend the cash he had obtained at the gas station. Torn between defiance and despair, I grabbed Elvis by the arm and insisted he at least open the trunk of the car so I could stash my pack inside. He did as I requested and then he was gone. I discreetly put my money belt inside my pack, closed it inside the trunk, locked all the doors of the car and perched myself on top of the trunk like a sentry.

Now I was at Ground Zero, and it didn't help that the sun was going down. This Cree reservation had been devastated by crack, crystal meth and alcohol. I felt like a fly in a spider's web. Even the wind had nothing to say for a change, and I wasn't of a mind to look around for a friendly encounter in these difficult surroundings. As if to confirm my apprehensions, flies buzzing in my face drew my attention to the rotting carcass of a maggot-infested housecat lying in the uncut grass 10 feet behind the car.

A woman of indeterminate age with a crooked nose that failed to line up with her lifeless eyes came by and tried to engage me in conversation. Her offer of a $5 blowjob was particularly repulsive as there was a child nursing from her sagging breast and a cigarette dangling from her toothless mouth. While I was trying to ignore her requests, a respectable mother was hurrying her children past this horrific scene. She paused long enough to cast me a look of total contempt. I felt falsely accused by proximity. Little did I know it was about to get a whole lot worse.

While I was distracted by this drooling druggie, a throng of people began to congregate on the hood of Elvis's car. By now it was getting dark and the mosquitoes joined the party. I nodded at the crowd at the other end of the car; while crude and rambunctious, they didn't appear particularly hostile. I was determined to hold my stance as gatekeeper on the trunk.

Suddenly the tenuous thread of normality was broken once again when a burly man with bulbous red eyes descended loudly towards me. His face was seething with righteous anger. He snarled an accusation close enough to give me the full benefit of his alcohol breath and a sharp thump on my chest. He then turned, viciously grabbed up his possession, Five-Dollar Mary, and her now wailing child and dragged them away like a caveman. I was completely rattled. When it comes to physical confrontations I am a coward; running away always works for me.

A little later I heard a squeaky clatter coming from the front of the car. The party crowd was removing the license plate, which I had recognized much earlier in the day to be Nova Scotia's emblem, the Blue Nose Schooner. Let 'em have it, I thought, as long as they didn't slash the tires or vandalize the vehicle, rendering it undriveable.

By now it had to be at least midnight, and the vampires and monkeys continued their vigil on and around the car. Their glassy eyes and hazy smoke in various shades and smells abounded throughout the night. Echoes of laughter and angry voices penetrated the darkness. Beyond fatigue and anger, I had started to doze off when I was startled back to consciousness by unexpected headlights illuminating by the now pitch-black night. I shaded my eyes and became aware that the high beams were attached to a pick-up with a flashing red light that was canvassing the blank stares of the vampires and monkeys.

Though no siren, the bright lights announced the arrival of the reservation police. Sure enough, out stepped the menacing presence of a short, dark-haired, barrel-chested man. He swaggered on over in his cowboy boots, and when he got a little closer, I could see a mean smile etched in his pockmarked face. When he barked out an order to produce my driver's license and registration I snapped to attention. I slid off the trunk and faced this bulldog in my best golly-gosh-gee-whiz way and tried to explain that everything I owned was locked inside my friend's car and I expected him back momentarily.

"You east coast boys coming out here to deal drugs, are you?" he snapped back at me like an old crocodile. I responded, "No, sir, I only drink beer." "Then you can afford to buy your way out of jail with $100 right now," he sneered. I knew better than to argue with this mixture of corrupt authority and the devil himself, but I couldn't produce the cash that might have eliminated this rodent because my money belt truly was locked in the trunk. I tried not to whine as I stalled, "No problem, as soon as my friend returns I'll be happy to oblige you with the $100 get-out-of-jail fee." Before my brain could catch up to my lips, I added, "Can I drop it off at the station?" As this lawless lawman stepped toward me he revealed raging black eyes. Also exposed was the criminal neglect of his own health with the unmistakable bad oral hygiene of a methamphetamine addict. As if I weren't already intimidated enough, his palm stroked the butt of his firearm holstered at his waist like the crazy cowboy he was.

"Apparently you're not familiar with reservation law. Let me educate you real quick. The station is right here, right now." He pointed to his outstretched hand. Not being able to produce the bribe money on the spot, my worst fears were materializing as I visualized myself being hauled off to jail and Elvis driving off with all my gear! Shit! What were my options?

I tried a shot at education myself by showing this extortionist that all the doors on the car were indeed locked. Then I inverted the pockets of my pants to expose the contents: Chap Stick, gum and $22 in cash. Thank God for mugger money. The drug deputy was not nearly satisfied with the menial amount of money I had, but he snatched it up anyway and retreated to his truck, grumbling a tirade of insults and threats.

I quietly said a little prayer for myself and the long-lost Elvis, hoping he was not shot, buried and forgotten. It reinforced my belief that nighttime was for vampires and monkeys and not for me. This was only the eighteenth day of an eighteen-month overland trip around the world. I was not even halfway across Canada and already getting my ass kicked. By the time the ribbons of sunlight were streaking the morning sky, no more confrontations had challenged my watch and Elvis finally returned.

He casually sauntered over and, without any explanation for his long absence, took his place at the wheel and turned the engine over. I was completely spent, bug bitten and still too spooked to give Elvis any grief over his disappearance. At the first truck stop outside the reservation I suggested we stop for coffee. Now it was my turn to point my feet in the opposite direction of this confused young man who was beyond anybody's help. I offered Elvis two more of my sandwiches and said goodbye.

My next ride could not have been more different from the turbulence of the night before. A young couple, also Canadian natives, was in the middle of a move to a new home. Although their pickup truck was stuffed with every belonging they had, they spent 10 minutes reorganizing the contents to make room for me in the back. Exhausted from the hell night, I periodically nodded off with the steady hum of rubber on the road. I happened to be awake when we passed a stranded Elvis pulled off to the side of the highway, clearly hobbled by his flat tire. Last night's scene was a serious wake-up call to always trust and act upon one's intuition.

Crack, crystal meth, & booze.

31
I Am What I Am

The mountains of Colombia are filled with waterfalls. The sound of cascading water is everywhere and is punctuated by the shrill laughter of exotic birds. The atmosphere is a thick distillation of heat, humidity and the sweet-and-sour smell of rotting vegetation. The sheer mass of the ecosystem can be an overwhelming attack on the senses. When I stood still and listened closely, it was as though I could actually feel nature growing and decaying simultaneously. Enormous trees stretch their rich foliage in every direction, producing an old-growth canopy. It blots out the sun in some places and in others lets beams of sun in, creating a masterpiece of light and shade.

I was on a long trek through the Amazon that had left me wet, bug-bitten, tired and at the threshold of my survival skills. The Amazon scraped and scratched the hell out of me with its prickly plants and thorny vines. After a month of traveling through this tropical terrarium, I was beginning to feel very claustrophobic. Now that I was in the mountains, I enjoyed the occasional respite near a waterfall, where the sky above the pool was open and the cooling effect of rapidly evaporating water lifted the veil of humidity.

I was hitching rides from truckers who were hauling goods and lumber from the small towns that border the jungle. Fifteen miles outside a town called Durada, the trucker who'd been kind enough to offer me a ride dropped me off and advised that the best place to camp and relax was a waterfall at a local park. His friend Maria, he boasted, had a restaurant at the base of the waterfall that served the best affordable food. The oasis and food sounded pretty good, so I thanked him and headed the couple of miles down the muddy mountain road towards the waterfall.

On the last bend before the entrance to the park, I secretly stepped off the road to rearrange my gear. I put together a daypack with a little food, headlamp, a book, swimming trunks and a sliver of soap to wash myself and the dusty clothes on my back. I put the rest of my gear in a black garbage bag and tucked it behind a tree out of sight from the main road.

Following the roar of water, I walked over a rise and paid the equivalent of a dollar to enter the quiet park. It was midweek, so the park was deserted. I went over to Maria's small thatch shack to bring her greetings from her trucker friend Carlos. Maria was a plump and gracious cook who was serving up spicy chicken tamales with beans and rice. The rhythm of Maria's chop, chop, chop and her daughter's pat, pat, pat shaping the soft corn dough immediately filled my fragile heart. It was like having my mother rub my back. These two women were as warm as their homemade tortillas, and I instantly decided to spend a few days there.

A small, rusty tin-roofed shack turned out to be the caretaker's lodging. The ancient custodian, Pedro, was friendly and skinny as a greyhound. Dark sacks hung beneath his eyes, perspiration beaded his forehead and his well-used smile looked like a rotten fence. Pedro told me that on this quiet Monday it was acceptable to wash my clothes and swim at the same time. I wandered over to the deep emerald pool that was collecting the colossal waterfall's overspray. I plunged into the refreshing pool and was immediately revived. Layers of road dust washed away and what I mistook for an amazing tan immediately dissolved. Freshly scrubbed, Pedro helped me find a good spot to dry my clothes. I sat down with him and shared my tin of sardines, which Pedro said was a welcome change from his simple diet of Maria's unsold tamales, scavenged berries and nuts, and the occasional river fish.

At five o'clock Maria, her daughter and a handful of other vendors closed their shutters and headed back to town. This is the time of day I like the best. On the bank of the river all things seemed to be in harmony as the sun slowly set. Feeling more secure, I returned to where I'd stashed my backpack and brought it to the park. I held up another tin of sardines and asked Pedro where I could put up my tent. He waved his arms expansively around and said in Spanish, "Tonight this place is yours; anywhere you like, my friend. We can cook your sardines with a bit of my rice." He stoked up the campfire and brewed a pot of coffee. Colombia is famous for its coffee, which is exported all over the world. However, it is next to impossible to get a strong cup of coffee in the country itself. Rich or poor, most Colombians drink very weak, sugary coffee and Pedro's was no exception, though a bit more flavorful with the smoke of the fire.

Pedro told me his story through the flickering flames as we ate supper and sipped coffee. His wife had long since died, and his two daughters were married and raising their children in the cramped quarters of Bogotá. He told me that in Colombia, retirement is a luxury for the rich. He didn't seem bitter but it was obvious that he was weary of working. That night as I lay in my tent listening to the roar of the waterfall I was reflecting on how I might spend my twilight years. "Is that how I'm going to go out," I wondered, "like the emaciated caretaker living in a tin shack and only eating meat by the grace of friends?" I was engulfed in loneliness so profound that it seemed like an impenetrable and inhospitable rainforest.

The beauty of being a bohemian wanderer is that one escapes the responsibility of planning life and allows it to just flow at the mercy of chance. But the price of sacrificing security comes when age begins to limit your ability to live like a whimsical breeze. At almost 50 was I getting too old for this game? As I fell asleep that night, I slipped into fretful dreams about the day I would be an increasingly limited wanderer and a burden.

At the break of a new day I was still pondering this mental crossroad and took a hike to the top of the incredibly beautiful and powerful waterfall. The exertion did wonders to restore my natural exuberance for living. When I returned to the pools in the early afternoon I met a young, bearded man who was coming down the road. He was dressed conservatively and wearing a well-used, dusty backpack. He introduced himself as Jack.

Jack was 27, from British Columbia and a graduate student who studied International Relations. He was 22 months into a two-year global trip. Jack's wanderlust had been stoked by the year he'd spent hosting "couch surfers" from around the world. It inspired him to step out and explore it for himself. Jack said his biggest observation in his travels was that "Canada is no different than any other country in the world; most all people gravitate toward being good, while most all systems such as business, churches, and governments are self-serving. The archaic yet proven methods for controlling the masses are still comfort, salvation, status and fear." I had to agree.

It was great hanging out with Jack, and we enjoyed swapping travel stories. He was so much like me with his aggressive optimism and love of people; we instantly bonded. Because of his interest in international relations Jack was politically in tune. We shared the view that "the west" had negatively impacted many third-world countries. "The western world," Jack explained, "exploits the desire of developing countries to obtain big, western-style economies by selling them extravagant infrastructure projects that they don't need and can't afford. Developers provide the engineering, the construction and the financing that it takes. Consequently, these countries find themselves in mounting financial debt and choking on the interest payments. Meanwhile, their people are further deprived of basic education and health resources so that these megaloans can be paid back." He added with a grimace, "It's not a service or a gift. Only the president of the country and his friends really benefit."

After a while the old caretaker Pedro came over, calling me "Marco," the nickname I use whenever I'm traveling in Latin America. Jack quickly won over Pedro by complimenting him on his baseball cap, a present I had given Pedro the day before. I had 10 more in my bag, purchased inexpensively at one of the many used clothing stores found around the world. The iconic baseball cap makes for a great American gift right off my head.

That night we borrowed Maria's big cooking pot and made our own version of "stone soup." Jack provided vegetables, Pedro provided rice and I added several tins of sardines. Pedro built the fire a little larger than usual so that it would last long into the night. The three of us shared miles of memories and created a few more beneath the Milky Way. In the morning we awoke to the smoky remains of the previous night's fire, more weak coffee and conversation. One life inspired another, and while Pedro represented a future where I may very well be headed, Jack represented the raw spirit of my youth: another planet-surfing vagabond. In the words of Popeye, "I am what I am."

Clean in Colombia

32
Central Africa

The misty mountains of central Africa are home to the silverback gorillas. Their tiny homeland borders the countries of Uganda, Rwanda and the Democratic Republic of Congo (DRC). This rainforest region is teeming with life. Its gushing emerald rivers and active volcanoes are some of the highlights of the fascinating geography. Much of Uganda is a tourist hotspot with cold beer, hot coffee and chocolate cheesecake. When I inquired about the silverback tour available there, I was told that the cost was $375 for 59 minutes of viewing time. The 40 people who were crowded around waiting for the day's tour to begin included an uptight German, a loud, angry Israeli couple and a chain-smoking Frenchman. I quietly left in hopes of finding a smaller and more interesting group the next day.

At a restaurant that night, I said to the Congolese waiter, "There are so many tourists here in Uganda. Why doesn't your country have any? Your border is open." "The Congo," he replied, "has so much gold, so many diamonds and so many warriors from different tribes. There is much political corruption so it isn't safe for tourists." The waiter then pointed up and over the mountain range and said in a beautiful French accent, "Ten miles from here is my Congo. We share the silverback gorillas with Rwanda and Uganda in the Virunga National Park that borders all three countries. It is a tiny park. On the Congo side, you can get the same tour for half the price you pay in Uganda."

The next day I paid $100 for a visa and crossed the border into the Democratic Republic of Congo. A tour guide standing next to his tired-looking Land Rover beckoned to me. Yuri was a Twa pygmy, who was tiny in stature but expansive in presence, and I liked him immediately. He had been giving gorilla and volcano tours since the '70s. I told him I was hoping to see the silverback gorillas and had little money. He drove me to his office and informed me that it was $250 with a $100 transport cost. I graciously thanked him for the offer but told him it sounded expensive and asked if I might share the transport cost with other tourists. Yuri said he didn't have any other tourists scheduled for another six days. When I stood up to thank him for his time, he suggested that I wait the six days and lodge at his "bed & breakfast."

After negotiating a price we drove out to his farm. It consisted of a few low buildings made of rough-cut lumber capped with rusty tin roofs. The area inside the compound was hard-packed earth. There were chickens, a milk cow and a large vegetable garden. I soon realized I was the first paying guest at Yuri's bed and breakfast.

Yuri prided himself on his perfect English and had passed on his language skills to his nine tiny children. The civil war of the '90s had been hard on both Yuri's family and country, but they were proud, well dressed and well educated. Three of Yuri's sons graciously moved into another very basic room in order to accommodate me. That evening we sat down to a great meal of beans and rice. During grace Yuri prayed for more tourists just like me. I found this pygmy family of 11 irresistible.

The next day, I followed the gang of kids to school on a squeaky borrowed bike to see their town. I did not spend much time at the farm during the day because Yuri's wife was the only one there. I could tell she was uncomfortable with me around, especially because she did not speak English and I spoke very little French. Consequently I spent a lot of time biking around. I was fascinated by how a quarter of the town was engulfed in cold black lava rock from a volcanic eruption in recent years. In the library I found a French edition of Dian Fossey's book, "Gorillas in the Mist," which I had read two months earlier. I was conscious of being the only white guy around, and everyone stared at me without smiling. I was not feeling the love and looked forward to 3:00 when my amazing family would return home from school.

Six days later and true to his word, Yuri picked up another tourist who was eager to see the silverbacks. John was a successful fishing boat captain from Alaska and was a giant in contrast to the stature of my petite friends. Yuri had already confided to me that since he and I were now old friends, I was not obligated to pay the $100 transport cost. We drove the short distance to Virunga where we met the general of a militia who was responsible for protecting the gorilla sanctuary. Accompanying the general were two armed soldiers and a barefoot pygmy tracker whose feet were as wide as they were long. Was this guy truly a general? I didn't know but he happily took our 500 dollars. The general showed us around the basic encampment with Yuri translating French to English for Giant John and me. He explained that because of hunters, poachers and human encroachment, soldiers were needed to protect the gorillas. This was my kind of expedition: more locals than tourists, a high-ranking corrupt official, and a pygmy tracker!

Giant John cast a nervous glance my way as our four-foot-tall pygmy tracker led us away from the main trail. We started bushwhacking through steep, unforgiving foliage climbing hand over hand. We were being led directly to the gorillas through radio contact with soldiers who track them. After two sweaty hours of hiking and feeling a little skeptical, we came upon two more heavily armed soldiers and shortly thereafter they led us to a band of 12 gorillas.

"Gorillas in the Mist" did not prepare me for my first encounter with these massive humanlike creatures. This particular band had one huge male, four females, many juveniles and two babies. Accompanied by a million flies, they munched reeds of bamboo, delicately stripping the stems of their sweet leaves. It was about one o'clock, the time each afternoon when the band lies down for a few hours before moving to their next camp.

We were allowed to get within 60 feet of the beautiful gorillas, but to my amazement and excitement, half of the band came closer. As the gorillas surrounded us, we watched them watching us. The littlest one had the nickname "Hats" because of his fascination with hats. Hats began climbing Giant John's leg in an attempt to get his hat. The big fisherman squealed as Hat's protective mama approached. To relieve the tension the pygmy tracker jumped in and pushed the baby closer to his mama.

Minutes later, the hair on the back of my neck rose as a major confrontation broke out between the huge male silverback and one of his female partners. In half a second he was on his feet and on top of her, raging in her face. In response to his vicious scolding, she avoided eye contact and submissively lay on her back. The male then returned grumpily to his place amongst his harem and cast threatening glares in her direction. The passing storm of the situation was so emotionally packed it left me trembling. The walk back out of the park was a quiet one as Big John and I processed the afternoon's events.

After 20 days I left the Congo, crossed another border and entered the strange little country of Rwanda. Rwanda is the most densely populated country in all of Africa, with a staggering 300 people per square kilometer. It has a typical colonial history that ended very poorly. The Germans colonized Rwanda in 1890, and the Belgians took it from the Germans as a prize after World War I. Both countries used the Tutsi tribe to their advantage. The Tutsis are a tall, beautiful tribe, quick to learn and made good administrators. In 1956, the Tutsis wanted their country's independence so the Belgians switched their allegiance to the Hutu. The Hutu represent the majority of the population by a six-to-one margin. In their newly found power the Hutu were hostile toward the Tutsi. In 1962 Rwanda won its independence from Belgium. Still in power, the Hutu limited the Tutsis' opportunity for education and work and forced many of them into Uganda. The Tutsi retaliated by raiding over the border at night. This caused a Hutu/Tutsi conflict in Rwanda and the surrounding countries that lasted over 30 years.

Political change ripped through the African world in the 1990s, bringing with it starvation and civil war. No country was harder hit than Rwanda. In 1994, after the Hutu president of Rwanda, Juvénal Habyarimana, was assassinated, the Hutu began arming themselves for a genocidal war against the light-skinned Tutsi. Over a period of one hundred days, beginning in June of

1994, Hutu militias murdered 800,000 Tutsi in an orgy of violence. That's 8,000 men, women and children a day being killed! When I visited three years later, the entire country was still in shock.

During my time in Rwanda I met a young man, perhaps 20 years old, named Junto. His ethnic background was mixed Tutsi and Hutu. He rented me a room at his family's hotel and told me how he survived the genocide. When it began in 1994, Junto's father, a Tutsi hotel owner, had to regularly pay off Hutu soldiers with money, food and alcohol to ensure his family's safety. When his reserves ran out he offered their furniture, which was refused, and then he was murdered in front of his own children. The following morning before dawn, Junto and his sisters sought refuge in the now-famous Hotel Rwanda.

The hotel had been abandoned by its owner and was doubling as a refugee center. Junto and his sisters lived in one of the rooms among the few hundred other Tutsi seeking asylum. They spent several weeks there rationing their food and using the pool for drinking water. During the course of their stay, Junto befriended an old, prestigious Tutsi lawyer who resided on the third floor. Junto and his sisters helped the kind lawyer with his daily chores.

Hutu soldiers showed up a month later and promised the refugees living in the hotel that they would be given safe passage to Kigali airport. The soldiers filled up a school bus with the first round of Tutsi residents from the hotel and drove off. Later the soldiers returned to pick up more of the remaining residents. Junto was horrified to note the blood and the shoes of fellow Tutsis left behind on the bus. He grabbed his sisters and hid in the old lawyer's room. Junto was emotionally recounting the dreadful details of his survival with tears stinging his eyes while crediting the old lawyer for saving their lives.

Sitting in his dark Victorian hotel lobby and listening to the detailed account of Junto's heartwrenching story, I learned firsthand that political upheaval scars many lives. The civil war of the Congo and the genocide of Rwanda made me happy to be back in Uganda, talking to my favorite Congolese waiter, sipping coffee and eating chocolate cheesecake.

33
Hitching Japan

This was to be the biggest trip to date, 26 months around the world. I left the U.S. on August 23, 2011, five months after the Japanese tsunami. Having viewed the shocking live footage on television, I vowed to help out in Sendai, Japan for a month. It had been a dozen years since my last visit to Japan. Upon arrival I cringed at the $100 train fare for the thirty-minute ride from the airport into Tokyo. Thank God the visa was free.

At rush hour I found myself swimming upstream in the exodus of Japanese suits making their way home. The street noise echoed off the glass and chrome of the massive skyscrapers. I was surrounded by the neon theatre of billboards with constantly changing digital rainbows advertising in a language I couldn't understand. Its font looked like spaghetti thrown against the wall to me.

I had once read in a Japanese guidebook that camping was permitted to pilgrims in any temple for one night. I found one such tiny old temple in downtown Tokyo. It was a small, raked-pebble garden with potted fruit trees, like a forgotten flower in a sidewalk crack. Generally I would have waited until sunset to set up camp, but I was extremely jetlagged and needed sleep. An Anglo backpacker didn't appear to warrant much attention from the pedestrians until I started erecting my tent on the pebble garden. Many a passerby stopped to stare at this recreational outlaw. It soon got to the point that I became a spectacle even to the road traffic. A $15-a-day budget limits my choices, so it was the comfort of my tent or nothing at all. I pretended not to be embarrassed as I hid my nose in my fat "Shogun" book.

Very early the next morning, a friendly hotel staff helped me write my cardboard Sendai hitchhiking sign in Japanese, gave me free tea and thanked me for volunteering. Then I took a public bus to the outskirts of Tokyo and began to hitch. Standing on the entryway to the highway going north, I waited and waited and waited. Not only did people not pick me up, they seemed to be laughing. Five hours went by and I was furious. Finally, a little beater Honda pulled over. Out of the car sprang a long-haired Japanese hippie in a 7/11 shirt. He came over to me carrying a magic marker and more cardboard. In very basic English he said thank you for volunteering. He showed me that I had been holding my sign upside down for the last five hours! With his thick magic marker he wrote a second cardboard sign in Japanese: "I am a volunteer."

The next day and a few hitchhikes later, my newest ride came to a closed road that headed up the coast where the nuclear power plant had melted down. We sped around the radioactive site. The driver nervously rolled up his windows and wore a two-dollar dust mask as he raced through this section of the highway without stopping. We were only 40 miles away and downwind of the still-leaking nuclear catastrophe!

A few days later I was dropped off in "tentville," where there were 200 tents full of volunteers, mostly college students from Tokyo. I spent a week with more long-haired cool cats cutting out sheetrock, fiberglass and filling up dump trucks with wet, black, moldy debris from the tsunami of five months earlier. The work was hard and dirty. Everyone smelled of bleach. A few of the students could speak English, and the energy was young and festive. The next week I spent helping a sweet, proud family clear out the incredibly huge mess in their house. A neighbor's car had smashed through their glass wall and floated into their living room. Dozens of neighbors in the community had drowned and washed out to sea. Everyone was still in shock.

It is because of unpredictable catastrophes like this that inside my left upper arm is a tattoo, which reads: "Kevin M. McNally 3.6.60 USA." I got the tattoo after experiencing an earthquake in Peru in 2007. I watched people rummaging through the pockets of dead bodies. Some were looking for loved ones, while others were looking for loot. If I died and someone stole my money belt, I would simply be another John Doe. I came to the conclusion that coming home in a body bag would be hell for my family, but not coming home at all would be much worse.

The lower part of the Sendai had simply been bulldozed over after the 100-foot tsunami wave rolled over the city in 2011. I am a Pisces and a lover of beauty; all this brokenness was beginning to crush my head. After some more solo volunteering I started working with the Billy Graham people. The kind middle-aged volunteers were enjoyable to work with and they had amazing western food. After a month of wrestling wet, moldy building materials I decided to head for Mount Fuji.

Late-September camping is spectacular in the Fire Lake region of Fugigoko with Mount Fuji looming large on its horizon. With an altitude of over 12,000 feet, this snowcapped volcano is the highest of Japan's three Holy Mountains and is an incredibly steep hike. Along the rigorous and rocky climb there are stations with holy men who brand hikers' Fuji walking sticks with symbols. Way before dawn I was hiking the northern ridge of Mt. Fuji with hundreds of ecstatic high school students. The morning was cold and clear with a small moon and lingering stars. I was surprised at the mental concentration, fitness and dedication of many of the students who, along with me, saw the summit before sunrise. The students were enthusiastic and animated in capturing me with their friends in hundreds of staged photos. In Asia I use the name Kay, which is easily pronounced, and my new best friends used it hundreds of times. Ancient Japanese proverb: Anybody would be a fool not to climb Mount Fuji once, but a fool to do so twice.

The following week I was in the back of a truck, traveling through dozens of hairpin switchbacks to go up and over the Japanese Alps. The low-lying mist and the twisted weathered pine trees outlining the panorama made it feel like a connection between heaven and earth. Hiking and camping in the stunning scenery of the Japanese Alps was nothing short of spectacular even in the cold rainy weather. Noticing more turbulent weather heading my way, I quickly disassembled camp, foolishly burying my rain pants deep in my pack, and set off for the road.

Heading towards the city of Kyoto, I was picked up just before the weather broke. Many soggy days in the woods did little for my appearance, but my new friend welcomed me eagerly into his luxurious Lexus. Its heated leather seats seemed to increase the aroma of my 10-day camping trip. My luck was perfect. Ten minutes into the ride the black cloud opened and the windshield wipers couldn't keep up with the torrent of rain. My cut-in-half Fuji stick was the topic of conversation for the first awkward 15 minutes with my executive friend. The walking stick symbolizes the Japanese holy mountain and with absolutely no language in common it seemed to give us a little connection.

Discerning that my driver wasn't going all the way to Kyoto, I began digging for those rain pants buried in the bottom of my pack. This well-dressed professional was amused rather than offended by the twigs, leaves and other wet crumbs of the Alps falling out into our laps. I think he felt terrible that he couldn't drive me all the way to Kyoto, and he kept insisting on something that I couldn't understand. During the next half hour of the ride I repacked and put on the rest of my rain gear, showing him that I was used to bad weather. I repeatedly told him that I was not in need of his enormous golf umbrella. I was surprised when he got out of his car and came around for a formal departure bow that left him soaked to the bone in seconds. As he drove off, the massive mahogany shaft umbrella clattered to the ground. When I opened it up, it began raining yen. "Hallelujah! It's raining yen!" I yelled as I ran down the street to collect the soggy blowing bills. Holy shit, there's one hundred dollars worth of yen here, enough for a bus into Kyoto and then some, I thought. Apparently the Japanese take gift giving really seriously.

Joining the permanent homeless for a week, I pitched my tent under the main bridge in the ancient town center of Kyoto. I was wet and cold and in need of a bath, so I splurged with the rest of the gifted yen on a visit to the famous Sento, one of the oldest bathhouses in the world. Even though I wasn't sure of the protocol I paid my money, took a shower and followed the noise. Hiding my private parts with the tiny hand towel provided, I slinked into the public soaking area. Some men were getting massages on the hot wet marble floor, while most others were soaking in steaming tubs, some of them smoking and chatting. Looking around, I realized I was the only foreigner there. There were five steaming pools full of men and one empty pool. Feeling extremely self-conscious and entirely too big for that small towel, I headed for the empty pool and noticed the conversation stop. I was feeling like a puppet on display and decided I had to act. I threw my towel aside and jumped in, instantly screamed and scurried out of the water. I stood there in shock. I had just electrified myself in freezing cold water. This pool was wired with electrical currents, which is apparently good for arthritis (or so they say). Everyone roared with laughter while I stood naked and stunned. Thankfully, a gent with tattoos from head to toe walked across the bathhouse and took me to his pool. The Japanese call this social experience of soaking "skinship."

Kyoto is Japan's city of traditional culture. The 1,200-year-old Imperial city boasts 1,600 Buddhist temples and 400 Shinto shrines. It has cobblestone streets, and bamboo and fruit trees are in every Zen garden. Kyoto also features numerous UNESCO (United Nations Educational, Scientific and Cultural Organization) World Heritage Sites. For a place to receive this special UNESCO title an international committee votes to make sure the site meets criteria proving it to be a "masterpiece of human creative genius." There are about 1,000 UNESCO sites in the world, and Kyoto has 17 of them! I spent a glorious week exploring many of these masterpieces.

Kyoto, Japan

Hitchhiking sailing boats, Nile River, Sudan

Hitchhiking with hunters in Alaska

Climbing "The King and I", Thailand

My transportation collection at age 23

34
Atlantic Crossing

This is a windy tale that starts 600 miles off the coast of Africa over the Cape Verde Basin. Two hundred days into an overland trip, I left the desert coast of West Africa and boarded *The Legend of Oz*, a 45-foot sailing sloop. The same thought kept coming back to me: Desert dunes and ocean waves are so similar yet so completely different.

The *Oz* with our crew of four men had been successfully zipping along with the help of the trade winds. Suddenly the winds stopped. After 24 hours of drifting without a hint of a breeze, Brian, a 21-year-old Irish adventurer on board as a deck hand, and I finally talked the captain into allowing us to swim alongside the boat. The charts told us we were in 23,040 feet of water, more than four miles deep! As we swam on the surface with masks and snorkels, Brian dropped a euro coin and we timed its waffling descent in 10 feet of water to calculate how long it would take to hit bottom. It would take 90 minutes for the euro to reach the ocean floor! Africa was 600 miles behind us and South America was 1,400 miles ahead. It was hard to believe we were swimming in the middle of the Atlantic because the calm waters resembled more of a glassy, windless lake than that of a vast ocean.

Captain Bill was a stout, seasoned sailor and bore a close resemblance to an English bulldog. His personality was completely altered by 10 days of sobriety. Bill's financier and partner had abandoned this voyage due to Bill's chronic alcoholism. On top of that Steve, the first mate, had insisted on a dry boat. The tension was high, and Captain Bill took his sober frustrations out on Brian and me, but we knew how to take orders in spite of his uneven balance of ego and spirit. It further irritated the Captain to see us frolicking in the calm seas. Despite the Captain's ill humor, he couldn't knock the shine off the two of us. Thank God for our companionship. As the tiniest wind began to stir, Captain Bill called us aboard to get the 'chute up. The 'chute is a sailing spinnaker, made of the finest, lightest fabric, similar to parachute material. This $5,000, multi-colored spinnaker was brand spanking new, a treasure the Captain had purchased in more prosperous days.

Bill and his sidekick Steve had begun shouting orders and criticizing our performance, calling us "the Irishman" and "the Yank." Brian and I followed orders even though there wasn't enough wind to justify hoisting the huge, new sail on the front of our small craft. The Captain chose this time to retire down below, but the wannabe captain was continuing to bark orders. With the wind backing off altogether, Steve made the decision to take the sail back down and continue to drift. It was tricky to find just enough wind in order to bag up the enormous sail without catching it on the shrouds.

I was listening for Steve's "Go!" command. Brian felt a whisper of wind and asked, "Now?" Steve's response was "No", but I heard "Go" and released the topping lift. Then I ran to the bow to help Brian stuff the sail as it came billowing down like an all-encompassing cloud. Steve began shouting, "Stop, stop" but it was too late as the delicate fabric of the new sail was impaled on the spreaders of the galvanized rigging. Drenched in fabric I didn't see the three-foot tear, which was enough of a gouge to render the sail useless and altogether broken. Bill came barreling up and stood naked in utter disbelief while I, not realizing it was stuck, was still trying to stuff the sail into its bag. When I noticed the resistance and stopped pulling, I turned to meet the murderous bloodshot eyes of the Captain. No one dared breathe a word, and the frothing, twitching Captain was incapable of speech. I attempted to stutter an explanation of what went wrong, but he sized up the situation and decided that I was to blame.

Grabbing a thin fillet knife in his reach and twitching like he had been electrocuted, the Captain descended towards the bow in my direction. Startled out of my shock, survival skills kicked in and I began evasive action to put space between the deranged Captain and myself. Fortunately, the boom and inflatable dingy made for a barrier in the middle of the deck and I used that to my advantage. I thought of diving overboard, but was sure he would leave me there. Captain Bill kept switching the eight-inch blade from right to left, as if trying to decide which hand he'd use to carve me up. In this zany game of tag around the zodiac, he found his voice and began a litany of insults beginning with, "Wipe that fuckin' smile off your face." Not wanting to antagonize the situation any further, I swallowed the smile I hadn't been aware of wearing. I began to realize that the naked Captain's macho attack was more show than an actual attempt on my life. I couldn't have been reduced any further in the detestable assessment of our fateful sober leader, but at least he was shrewd enough not to kill me!

A week later, on day 11, having left the placid waters of Cape Verde behind us, the mighty Atlantic resumed its majesty with 20-foot swells. With a thousand miles behind us and a thousand miles in front of us, we navigated the *Oz* west in the mighty rollers with punch and verve. Both the auto-helm and the refrigerator had broken on day one and the engine was moody. Daily catches were our meal ticket since our cold food storage had rotted.

Our reliable fishing rig was a hundred-foot line with a simple lure made of a red Coke bottle cap, a fishing hook and plastic streamers from a child's bicycle handlebars. From the surface, this bohemian lure sounded and looked strikingly like a squid. A can attached to the line and filled with screws acted as our alert when something took the bait. An old African fisherman had shared this secret with me, and it was first rate. He wisely imparted, "A fish, I'm fed; a line and a hook, I'm fed forever."

On this particular clear day, all the sails were out and we were riding the waves with intention at seven knots. In the immensity of the mighty sea, we hadn't spotted another vessel in days. I was alerted when I heard the rattling of the can and jumped up to haul in the line. The line, which had been trailing behind us, now took an aggressive lead, passing our boat. Bill barked out an order to cut the line so it would not get tangled in the propeller. Brian and I ignored the command as we took the initiative to capture this fighter. Hand over hand, with Brian tying up the slack, it took us a solid 20 minutes to retrieve the hundred-foot line back into the violently rolling boat. Our prize was none other than a 30-pound yellowfin tuna, two and a half feet long and as round as a basketball. Given our battle wounds from hand-lining this fish, I had respect for its muscular torpedo-like build. I held up our dinner to the delight of all but the Captain, who was blustering about blood on the deck. This dry drunk was never going to be satisfied with the "sail ripper" and the young Irish aristocrat. Right then and there, we prepared the delectable feast, which was no easy task in 20-foot rollers.

Going below to the galley and trying to cook on the gimbaled stove was next to impossible in this wild ride. It was not the terror of a ship on its beams end, but the constant rising and falling was unnerving. By sunset the rollers had doubled in size to 40-feet-big open sea swells! Thank God the storm was blowing true east to west. Every time we crested another mountain I could hear the shrouds whistling in the wind and the ominous groans of the hull being persecuted under its own weight. The little sloop fell into the next trough and it always seemed as if it might not recover. The voyage became a very long, arduous, scary and sleepless journey. We trimmed the sails full reef and prepared the best we could for the crazy night ahead.

During the day, you could anticipate the roller-coaster ride while at the helm, but at night with the shapeless dark waves you could only feel where you were on them, making it much harder to navigate. The boys and I fought to stay in our bunks through the beating. By midnight the frantic roll of the ship was unbelievable as the angry sea repeatedly fell upon itself with a crushing roar. Gear was spilled everywhere. I could hear Brian at the helm swearing into the night and the first mate Steve, half laughing, half crying. Brian called down to me to come take my watch.

I was thrown to the floor several times while putting on my foul weather gear. Staying upright proved too challenging on the pitching floor so I finally had to finish dressing while lying down. I grasped the handrail that led aloft and struggled up the narrow ladder. Not yet clipped into my safety line, I was welcomed by the drenching soak of a rogue wave. I clipped in next to Brian, and he explained the best approach to fight the monstrous waves. He had captured the boat's speed record at 16.2 knots. We talked for a few minutes, then he left me with his iPod. Dialed in to the music that he had downloaded for me, I began my watch with Led Zeppelin, Pink Floyd & Yes. I turned off all the deck lights in order to better see the dark ocean, and in the vastness of night with the motion of the rolling seas, I sat alone. The only thing lit was the compass rose.

I think sleep deprivation had a strangely narcotic effect upon my senses because I was calmer than I might otherwise have been in this crazy scenario. I wasn't afraid as I braced myself for the next plummeting descent into the abyss. The enormous waves rose at the command of the moon and wind, and I wondered if the little boat could take much more of this punishment. My senses were heightened to their utmost during this challenging watch.

The darkness of night turned slowly to the anxious dawn, and as the Milky Way was fading, so were the swells. Sometime during the night I surpassed Brian's record to boast a remarkable 16.8 knots. You must confront your fears in order to dissipate them, and having run the gamut of emotions, I felt triumphant that the *Oz* and her crew, including the grumpy sober captain, had prevailed victoriously over the Atlantic crossing. The following morning, over cold tuna and rice I said to my good friend Brian, "A ship is only safe in the harbor," to which he replied, "But that's not what ships are for."

Curious whale swimming under our sailboat, middle of the Atlantic

35

African Bushmen

Africa is one of those places that has sustained the time-tested relationship between man and nature. The sun streaks this vast continent in magical light, revealing the precarious balance of life and death for all its inhabitants. In my three years of camping in Africa, I grew to love the continent that has been host to some of my most remarkable adventures.

The unpaved roads in southern Africa are made up of very fine dust, much like the consistency of talcum powder. Everyone and everything is covered by this grime, and it often compromises respiratory health. When a truck passes and churns up the talcum powder, the dust can rise 30 to 40 feet in the air and it can take up to five minutes to completely resettle.

I spent three lovely days camping on the southern banks of the upper Limpopo River, doing laundry and swimming. I hadn't been so clean in months. Eventually, I started to look for a boat that would take me across the broad river. Brilliant blue kingfishers darted past as I walked along the southern bank in search of a dugout or a small ferry.

In the morning breeze, I met up with a tall, humming boatman who was as thin as his pole. I joined him and five children who were on their way to school. On the other side of the river was a tiny village of mud huts and a small cinderblock dwelling that served as the regional school. While I ate a breakfast of duck eggs and corn mash, a local man told me that three miles downriver was a town with a road that headed north.

Barking dogs announced my arrival as I approached the next town, which belonged to the Xhosa tribe. These tall, lanky people have bright, white teeth that contrast deeply with their black skin.

On the banks of the village a couple dozen women, mostly topless and all wearing colorful patterned skirts, were standing thigh high in the river doing their laundry. Every woman was standing beside her own table of stacked flat stones, which broke just above the water surface. They used wooden paddles to beat the clothing on the stone tables, and the sound was deafening.

I smiled as I walked by, waved both hands and practiced my Swahili greeting on them. They all stopped what they were doing and stared. Now the silence was deafening. One woman began slapping the water with her large, black hands in a rhythmic beat and most of the other women followed suit. Then she began a chant in a beautiful high-pitched voice and the other women harmonized their responses. It was my turn to be surprised, but I took it to be a courting song because the few young, wide-eyed girls who didn't participate in the singing giggled wildly.

Taking leave of this symphony, I headed up the hill towards town, where my attention was beckoned by the familiar red flag waving in the wind. It's Africa's version of advertising and an easily understood system. Merchants of all kinds display small, colored flags at their door: white for moonshine, blue for beer, red for wild game, and so on. I made my way towards the red flag advertising my favorite 'kudu jerky' and ducked inside a blackened smokehouse.

The woman inside was busy blending salt, sugar and various spices to coat the gamey meat. Hundreds of thin strips were hanging from rusty hooks woven with fishing line across the ceiling. The knack to choosing the best cured kudu rather than buying buffalo or other less preferred game is to find the driest section of hanging meats in the shop. Since the merchants don't provide containers I filled up my well-used Ziploc bag. Half the people in Africa live on less than two dollars a day, making them the ultimate recyclers!

In my clean clothes and with my pack well stocked with food and water, I headed for the road to continue my northbound journey. I climbed aboard a 10-wheel truck full of grain and re-entered the world of dust. Instantly the exterior layer of my world was once again covered in fine layers of soot. We were off and heading north and though I didn't speak the language, I made friends with four workers in the back of the truck by sharing some of the jerky. The sacks of grain I was lying on made for a comfortable journey as I watched the strange baobab trees in the passing landscape.

In the morning sun I was awakened from dozing by the shouts of my new friends who were heckling someone at the upcoming crossroads. Looking over towards the cause of the commotion, I saw to my amazement five small, brown Bushmen. These were the famous San tribe of Africa. I leapt suddenly for the cab of the rusty old truck and began drumming on the roof. The driver pulled over a quarter of a mile from where we had passed the Bushmen. I jumped down into the ankle-deep powder to pay my fare, and the dust storm once again enveloped us. Three of the truck riders immediately took refuge from the overwhelming dust storm by covering their faces with blankets. By mimicking bow-and-arrow shots at me, the one rider who braved the elements of the dusty squall warned me that these little men were very dangerous.

As the truck pulled away, I turned my attention back south to survey the five hundred feet that separated me from the tribesmen. I could envision what trepidation missionaries must feel when first probing the wilderness and encountering unfamiliar cultures and people armed with poisonous arrows. The next few minutes would either go very well or very badly! Although I couldn't see the Bushmen at the moment, concealed as I was in the dust blizzard, I didn't think a surprise appearance would be the best way to introduce myself.

Coming upon the intersection where I had spotted the tribesmen, I nervously began waving both hands and singing songs of greeting in an attempt at a peaceful first impression. While my heart was pounding, the mirage of warriors began taking shape. Three of the Bushmen were standing with arrows in their bows, though not drawn. Two others were hunched down with capes protecting their heads and stood up as I approached. These brown men, covered in dust, were less than five feet tall with sun-hardened wrinkles. Their garments were an interesting mix of loincloths and gourds covering their groin. They all wore earth-colored capes and were barefoot. Their hair, peculiarly light in color, was fashioned into half-inch twisted tuft balls divided by patches of scalp. I respectfully slowed my pace, still singing a greeting and waving congenially. I stopped about 70 feet away on the other side of the intersection, stared and mentally tried to relay my friendly intentions. Then I slowly took off my pack and sat on it, pretending to wait for another truck.

As the Bushmen continued to check me out, they began chattering using a combination of noises. Various clicking and kissing sounds mixed with throaty, guttural tones peppered their language. I had never heard anything even closely resembling this kind of communication and was utterly and absolutely amazed! For a good 10 minutes, they kept up this banter of guttural clucking, clicking and kissing sounds, presumably discussing who the hell I was.

Maintaining a friendly smile on my face for another half an hour, we continued gawking at each other and then I saw what it was that they had been waiting for at this spot. Another Bushman with his wife and baby sporting the same extraordinary hairstyle were coming down the crossroads. The mother's enormous buttocks served as a shelf for the baby to be carried upon. They greeted each other with clicks and kissing sounds and then all eyes were cast towards me, followed by more conversation.

They turned and walked into a land that seemed to stretch forever. I had spent an hour observing a culture completely alien to anything I've ever seen before. There were no more passing vehicles that day and it gave me plenty of time to think. By nightfall, I put up my tent and slept fitfully right there in the middle of the intersection. Thankfully, by ten o'clock the next morning the first northbound cargo truck of the day picked me up.

I thought about sharing the planet with tribes such as the San Bushmen. I am delighted to glimpse primitive groups, and I couldn't help but feel a little melancholy thinking that the previous day's encounter might be the climax of my African experience. This continent would be forever scorched in my memory and burnt into my heart. I wondered how many secrets she still had to offer.

36
Uncle Kev's Boot Camp

When my oldest brother, EJ, told me his 14-year-old son Ryan could use some guidance, I dropped my work and headed to Boston to pick up my nephew. Ryan was a good kid stumbling his way into his teens, and I hoped that spending some time together would help him find a smoother path. When I saw him looking around for me at the airport, I let him squirm a few minutes before going up and giving him a welcoming hug. From the airport we drove north to a friend's farm where I picked up a canoe and rock climbing gear. We headed over to the local Salvation Army used clothing store and for less than $30 Ryan had outfitted himself in traveling clothes. We were ready to go explore.

Dropping the canoe by the river and abandoning my car, we camped for the next six weeks. To start, we rock climbed 500-foot Cathedral Ledge in the White Mountains and then spent the rest of the first week canoeing 104 miles down the Saco River to the Atlantic Ocean. Continuing north, we hitchhiked inland through New Hampshire, Vermont and then Quebec.

At the U.S. border, the customs agents were skeptical of our hitchhiking expedition. They thought it was a bit reckless to take a fourteen-year-old kid hitchhiking through Canada. They separated us and questioned Ryan at length to verify that I was indeed his uncle and that he was going voluntarily. On the Canadian side we were greeted warmly, "You've come all the way from Florida to see our beautiful country!" An agent gave Ryan a Canadian pin for his oversized rain jacket and taught him a few words in French. The Canadian attitude was a refreshing contrast to our side of the border.

They also informed us that Quebec City was hosting an Indian powwow.

The two-day hitch to historic Quebec was sunny and rural. Hitching with a kid was fun because people couldn't do enough for us. I could see Ryan growing up before my eyes. At the powwow, we joined the Micmac Indians. They demonstrated how to start a fire using flint and how to weave baskets. They gave us a sample of their beaver-tail stew, which was delicious. We swapped stories with the Micmacs late into the night, and Ryan and I welcomed their offer to let us use a teepee for the weekend.

Then Ryan and I headed east through New Brunswick and Nova Scotia. On Cape Breton Island we were picked up by the owner of a recording studio, who invited us to sit in on a session. One of the musicians, a drummer, invited us over for the much appreciated "holy trinity of travelers" - a big hot meal, a long hot shower and laundry!

Next, we took the five-hour ferry to Newfoundland, a secluded island in the northern Atlantic and home to a very salty breed of oldschool mariners. Heading up the coast, we were picked up by a lobsterman named Bert Johnson. He took us on his boat the next day, and that evening we had a big feed of fish and lobster. After a hard day of labor, Ryan and I knew we had earned the respect and hospitality of the locals. Bert couldn't say enough about Ryan's work ethic. Bert's daughter was just about ready to head off to college. She was a friendly combination of Canadian small-town innocent and budding intellectual. She listened well and spoke with true insight. Ryan and I loved the Johnson family.

A few days later, we made it up to the very north of the island to a historic Viking village. A thousand years ago, a small band of Vikings spent a few winters at this very spot where native Indians, icebergs and whales were their neighbors. Ryan and I were adopted by the Viking reenactors at L'Anse aux Meadows, a UNESCO World Heritage Site. Cole, a short, bearded trader, taught us how to throw an axe. While becoming fairly adept at this Viking pastime, Ryan accidentally broke the handle. Cole talked Ryan through carving a new handle using a drawknife.

The weather was turning bad so Ryan and I spent the next day with the women tending the fire and making soup. There was a hard rain on the moss roof and yet it stayed so cozy inside the cabin. The women doing chores in their period costumes were dreamy. But the spell was broken when the reenactors rolled up their artifacts and went home for the evening at 5:00 p.m., leaving Ryan and me to make our way into a howling gale.

We took refuge under a flipped-over abandoned fishing boat with broken glass and stray cats. It was definitely a low point. Ryan was furious about the makeshift shelter and poor, smelly conditions so I said to him, "If you want to put up the tent in this pouring rain, go for it, I'm fine here." To my astonishment Ryan put on his headlamp, started organizing his pack under the old boat and slid out into the hard rain. He came back in, grabbed the rest of the gear and called me ten minutes later when my bed was made. Ready or not, this fourteen-year-old rich, suburban kid had found a new puzzle piece in life and was turning out to be a resourceful young man. That night Ryan read the highlights of our journey to me from his journal. Childhood is the one journey that stands by itself in every soul. After six weeks on the road together, I'm not sure whether it was the over-sized boots or the 20-pound moose antler tied to his pack, but Ryan looked a couple of inches taller!

Ryan's experiences on our six-week expedition remind me of a quote, which is as relevant today as it was a century ago: "an important side of sport should be simple life: to come a little away from the many, away from the confusing noise, where we live our lives to an ever greater degree, to come out into nature, get new and grander impressions from forest and fields, from the wide plains, from the great open spaces. City life is now, for one thing, anti-nature. When these people look for relaxation and new impressions, it would make sense for them to search for something far from this city life and in the place where they originally belonged: God's great, wide open nature." -excerpt from Norwegian Arctic explorer and statesman Fridtjof Nansen's speech at the Norwegian Tourist Association's meeting for youth in 1921.

37
Songs of Freedom

A Scandinavian girl named Britta had teamed up with me in Mexico. Two months of hitching from the tops of cargo trucks through Guatemala, El Salvador, Honduras, Nicaragua and Panama was a marvelous, easy-going way for us to view Central America.

At the Panama Canal Britta and I were parting ways. The next three-week leg of my journey was walking the Darien Gap from southern Panama to northern Colombia, after which Britta and I planned to meet up again in Cartagena, Colombia. At the moment my priority was to help her secure a safe passage by boat to Colombia.

The seedy old town and duty-free port of Colón had a dangerous reputation. We bribed our way onto the commercial wharf, which was a high-traffic area for all sorts of contraband, and immediately sensed a pirate-like quality to its underbelly. Nonetheless, we set about soliciting cargo boats and freighters docked at the many rows of piers, but weren't getting any takers that seemed safe. Britta and I were feeling dispirited until we came across a small, wooden cargo boat among all the steel giants.

This old 120-foot, leaking working boat had both bilge pumps running. She hailed from the homeport of Kingston, Jamaica. The *Miss Kingston* was used to run basic goods from Panama back to Jamaica. Britta and I were invited aboard *Miss Kingston* by her charismatic captain, a man with a huge white smile framed by a very black face. The wheelhouse was steamy with the smell of plantains, beans and rice cooking on a makeshift stove. We were offered big plastic cups containing a mixture of fresh-squeezed grapefruit, water, sugar and rum. Although the *Miss Kingston* wasn't able to provide us transport to Colombia, her crew was happy to party with us. An hour into great conversation with the crew, a truck delivered large cardboard boxes of cheap toilet paper and we all swung into action to load it. Using the bucket brigade system, we made short work of dropping the lightweight boxes down to a sweaty Rasta who carefully added the new cargo to the already half-full hold. "With a leaky boat like *Miss Kingston*, dry cargo like this gets the best seat in the house," the captain said with hearty laughter. While working we sang snippets of Bob Marley songs that played righteously in the background.

Britta and I were having a great time, grooving to Marley, working, enjoying the rum and laughing at the Jamaicans' attempts at flirting with her. The festive mood was broken like a scratch across vinyl when a strange parade of vehicles emerged onto the compound from the gatehouse. A truck full of soldiers and an army Jeep were followed by a black stretch limousine with two state flags signifying the arrival of a dignitary. The tension mounted as the convoy took a hard right onto our pier and headed straight towards us. It reached a boiling point when armed soldiers jumped out of the truck with our small party in their sights. The officer in charge was frantically waving his pistol around and in a demanding voice ordered us to line up on the pier with our hands behind our heads. Two additional armed men rushed past us and boarded the *Miss Kingston*. Marley was still playing in the background.

The black tinted window of the limo lowered noiselessly and from the interior a suited arm emerged, adorned with a gold cufflink, a bulky gold bracelet and a giant gold ring on a finger of the hand. The excitable officer in charge, still blustering in Spanish, stopped in front of me with his pistol trained at my chest and demanded my passport. I slowly lifted my shirt and fished out my passport from my money belt while maintaining eye contact with this high-strung official. Meanwhile, two soldiers who were clad from head to toe in full-on SWAT gear dumped out our packs.

My pack contained camping gear and dirty clothes and oh shit, several small packages of dried hummus in clear plastic bags.

Months earlier, for space considerations, I had taken the hummus bags out of the original boxes, intending to eat it on my upcoming trek through the Darien Gap. It didn't occur to me that dozens of clear plastic bags of dehydrated hummus might look a lot like bags of heroin. The whole conflict turned on a pin when the soldiers grabbed up the dried hummus bags and began shouting in excitement. I was fluent enough in Spanish to know that a big mistake was in the making, but I wasn't conversant enough to explain the complexities of the situation. The rising sense of panic hit me like lightning; I had to act or risk getting caught up in a corrupt justice system with no easy outs. I held my breath and made the snap decision: Do or die, or maybe, do and die!

I ducked around the crazy armed officer and in an instant was running towards my pack. The soldiers were shouting and I sensed rather than saw that several guns turned their aim on me. Intent on my purpose, I ignored them and dropped to my knees. I grabbed for one of the packets of dried hummus and frantically ripped it open with my teeth and began devouring it like a monkey on meth. I nervously inhaled some of the powder and instantly went into a coughing fit. Losing all sense of my limited Spanish skills and dignity, I spit out the words, "Food! Food! Eat! Eat!" The hummus was sticking all over my sweaty, bearded face and my terrified eyes were watering. Still on my knees, coughing and trembling, I wondered if they understood that this was food. The time seemed to stretch out forever before I finally heard a deep laugh from inside the limo. The tension was broken as the "golden hand" returned our passports to the officer in charge. The two soldiers presiding over me turned their rifles towards the sky. Yes! They got my message. I was safe!

While trying to regain my composure, my eyes so watery I could hardly see and my face still covered in the powdery hummus, the soldiers were having a laugh at my expense. Then they turned their attention away from Britta and me and began shaking down the Jamaicans. The deep commanding voice of the anonymous authority inside the limo indicated that Britta and I could take our leave. You have never seen two people pack so fast.

Britta and I quickly walked away from *Miss Kingston*. We turned and waved farewell to the wide-eyed crew with their hands behind their heads. The seasoned captain smiled in return, but no one dared wave back. As we left the compound Britta and I hummed to Marley's "Redemption Song," which we could still hear playing from the old wooden boat. I don't fear death but I do so love life and the more I live, the more I just wanna be able to keep on singing!

Boys posing for beautiful blond Britta, Panama City, Panama

38
On Safari with Mom

Three extra Delta Airlines buddy passes came my way one year, so Mom, my younger brother Michael, and my wonderfully optimistic brother-in-law Craig decided to join me on a safari in South Africa. Discounted tickets work only when stand-by seats are available, so, as a gift, they are something of a double-edged sword. When my family was to arrive, I had already been in South Africa for a month and a half on my way to Egypt. For three nights in a row I wandered the Johannesburg airport waiting for them to arrive. I love the international flavor of this airport. A favorite pastime of mine while waiting at Jo'burg airport is trying to decipher people's country of origin. I met a porter who had tribal scars and slashes all over his face, which I found both obscene and fascinating. I couldn't take my eyes off of him. You would have thought he went through the windshield of a car except that the scars were symmetrical. He told me that he was from Chad. His scars had been made by a medicine man who used a razor to cut his skin and then mixed animal fat and ash and put it into the wounds to make them more pronounced. "It drives the country girls wild," he said with perfect teeth showing through a divine smile.

A dozen Zulu dancers of enormous stature were performing a tribal war dance in an alcove of the airport. I passed a security guard, peeked in and found, to my surprise, that they were performing for the Dalai Lama. The Dalai Lama was with a young Tibetan man and they were both outfitted in traditional maroon Buddhist robes. In contrast, the Zulu warriors were adorned in costumes of animal skins, feathered headdresses, spears and shields. For several minutes the drummers pounded out a beat that kept the warriors bouncing and thrashing, their frenzied dance style symbolic of warfare. The Dalai Lama watched with a gentle smile on his face. At the end of their performance he put his hands together and gave a slight bow to each of the dancers. It appeared that the South Africans didn't understand the gesture so he walked around the circle and shook hands with each one.

Like half the world, I was awestruck by the Dalai Lama so I placed myself at the middle of the receiving line for a handshake with him. This god among men, whose life has inspired so many, exited through a back door and was gone. A six-foot beauty with an ostrich feather headband and dripping with sweat standing next to me asked, "Who was that?" I stared at her incredulously and replied, "Why, the Dalai Lama. He's like the pope of Asia."

An hour later my family finally came out of the gate and my mother announced that her luggage had been lost. "Good," I said with a laugh and a hug, "It's best to lighten your load and go native, Mom, plus our rental car is really small." I shared the amazing events of my encounter with the Dalai Lama and the African dancers as we headed for Kruger National Park.

At Kruger we dined in one of the huge, open-air pavilions with woven thatched roofs and we slept in elegant bungalows. The food and service were excellent. It was an oasis of good taste and serenity in the heart of Africa. The size of Israel, Kruger is the best animal observatory in the world, and what makes it unusual compared to other game reserves in Kenya and Tanzania is that you can drive your own car inside the park. It is also host to the "Big Five": lions, leopards, elephants, cape buffalo and black rhinos. You can also observe cheetahs, giraffes, hippos, impalas, zebras, blue wildebeests, kudus, waterbucks, baboons and hundreds of other species. A memorable encounter occurred the first day when an enormous bull elephant was walking through the bush and our car got too close to it. The elephant stamped his feet, flared his ears and trumpeted a warning, which we quickly heeded.

The next day we were in the grasslands on the savannah. My brother Mike was driving way too fast on a single-track road.

Speeding around a corner we suddenly came upon a mother rhino nursing her baby in the middle of our path. Mike slammed on the brakes and slid sideways to avoid hitting them. Mama Rhino immediately gave chase. Mike threw it in reverse as we all screamed wildly. It seemed like an eternity before we outdistanced, in reverse, the charging, mad mama and then we proceeded to calm down our own mad mama. Although our full-speed retreat was a testament to Mike's reverse-driving skills, Craig was elected to drive for the remainder of the day.

We saw a family of hyenas resting in the afternoon heat. While the adults were sinister looking and kind of creepy, the youngsters were adorable. The hyena is actually less scavenger-like than its foe the lion, and mother hyenas will use their long, sharp incisors to painstakingly strip the meat from bones to lovingly feed their young.

Several days into the safari adventure we finally saw three young male lions at dusk. They approached our car with the stealth and aloofness of the average house cat. With the illusion of safety in our rented car, only 10 feet separated us from the Kings of Africa. They eyed us with a detached curiosity that made me feel like the spectacle. Their glorious manes were the same golden color as their eyes and as breezy as the waving golden grass on which they stood. These animals were as vivid as the scarlet sunset behind them and will be forever emblazoned in our memories.

From Kruger we moved on to the kingdom of Swaziland, the smallest country in Africa. I could feel the racial tension from South Africa dissipate as soon as we crossed the border. With only one ethnic race and nothing in the way of resources to extract, this poor country hadn't been colonized by Europe. In contrast to South Africa, the atmosphere was one of warmth and relaxed friendship.

We went to Mlilwane Wildlife Sanctuary and stayed at the Sondzela Backpacker Lodge, the self-proclaimed Rolls Royce of hostels. It came highly recommended to us by fellow travelers and had a rate of $10 per night, which included a great breakfast. My 70-year-old mother fit in perfectly with the international community and she had the ability to strike up a conversation with everyone she met. Taking turns cooking and sleeping head to toe in the dorm was no problem for this mother of seven. Mom and I woke up very early to take our ceremonial coffee in the backyard. One morning we spooked two zebras drinking from the swimming pool and they bolted off toward the misty Mdzimba Mountains.

We told our bunkmates that today's mission was to drive into town and find the palace to meet "the King." King Mswati III was crowned in 1986 at age 18. He is the second of 67 sons and has 200 siblings. Mswati is one of the last three remaining monarchs in Africa, most likely because his ancestors fought off the Zulus and Boers and later the British. Mswati declared a five-year sex ban for teenage females in an attempt to curtail the AIDS epidemic in his country. Two months later he married a 17-year-old! There was such an outrage that he was forced to lift the ban. Mswati himself has 14 wives and countless offspring. Even though we didn't find the king, it was still a great day.

Later we headed up the hill from the hostel and found a bohemian outdoor restaurant with a safari camp flavor. This would be our final meal together and we were feeling jubilant about our trek across this sun-scorched continent. Mike and I ordered boar, while Mom and Craig opted for the kudu. Giant slabs of wild game cooked to perfection combined with the black cherry flavors of robust South African wine helped us to celebrate in style. The next morning we said our goodbyes while standing in the red soil, which contrasted with the herd of black-and-white striped zebras surrounding us. I watched my family drive south to the airport, then turned and headed north to continue my long overland journey to Egypt.

"You can kiss your family and friends goodbye and put miles between you but at the same time you carry them with you in your heart, your mind, your stomach, because you do not just live in the world but the world lives in you."

-Frederick Beuchner

39

The Holy Man by the River

After spending two serene months with mild temperatures high in the Nepalese Himalayas, the weather conditions in northern India seemed stifling hot. I found the archaic cargo boats anchored along the sandy banks of the holy Ganges River absolutely fascinating. These rough-planked working boats are about 70 feet long and 20 feet wide. Their design is so efficient that it has not changed in hundreds of years.

I was lucky enough to hitchhike on one such boat carrying wood destined for funeral cremations in Varanasi. It was a little difficult to get comfortable on the stacks of twisted dried trees. The large cargo boats use sails to navigate upstream, but going downstream fully loaded like today's trip, they are better maneuvered with oars. The unpredictable river wind required four men at the long oars even with the help of the strong current. The young captain stood at the huge tiller and steered us away from the shallow banks. In the hot sun, the cadence of the oars combined with the rhythmic grunts of the oarsmen, and the captain's dark, watchful eyes made me feel like a lazy tourist.

We were coming into the oldest living city in the world and in the way many a traveler has entered throughout the ages: by way of the river. The glittering stars came out in force that night and then were dulled with the finest slice of a late-rising crescent moon. Two of the oarsmen slept while the other two steered the course. The captain let me take the tiller while he ate and brewed a cup of tea. There I was, steering an ancient boat with wood intended to blaze the bodies of deceased pilgrims, which would set their souls free!

The morning woke with a fiery red sky and the captain told me we were getting close. When the Ganges turned sharply, I could see the beginnings of the holy city. The river's long course descends from the Himalayas all the way to the Bay of Bengal. The Ganges is believed by the Hindus to hold the power of salvation in every drop. Each year Varanasi welcomes millions of pilgrims. Pilgrims, by definition, are travelers who journey to a holy place for religious reasons. Hindu pilgrims seek salvation on the entire Ganges River, but Varanasi is by far the busiest and the holiest destination on its riverbanks.

Thousands of pilgrims were bathing in the soft, golden light of early morning. The captain told me there were 70 *ghats* in a four-mile stretch, marrying the great Hindu city to the river. "Ghats," he explained, "are stone steps built on the embankment and leading down into the river so that worshippers can bathe." As we docked at a "burning ghat," which was used for funeral cremations, I was greeted by the faint smell of singed hair and sandalwood and the sounds of gongs, bells and prayers. I grabbed my pack and stepped into the ancient city in search of lodging. The noisy streets were teeming with color, and the air hung heavy with humidity. Most everything in Varanasi makes you look twice!

A funeral procession passed and forced me into a recessed entryway. The narrow maze of lanes and alleys was daunting. It was easy to get lost, so it was calming to know that the river was always close by. The city's buildings ranged from shanty to shrine and the alleyways hid a disorderly array of eighteenth-century palaces. After a few wrong turns I found a crumbling sandstone palace, which had been transformed into an international hotel.

My knock at the hotel door was answered by a beautiful young woman in a flowing purple sari. The hostess spoke in perfect English and invited me into the elegance of the foyer. The stunning chandelier was mostly intact, but the focal point was a magnificent white marble staircase that positively glowed in the pink sandstone interior. A regiment of fanning peacocks carved from marble spiraled up the four-story staircase. The hostess told me that all the rooms had been taken but I could sleep on the roof for a dollar if I didn't mind the late-night music.

The roof was littered with travelers who had settled for a $1 a spot, and from it was a magnificent view of hundreds of colorful kites dotting the skies. A German hippie was playing his guitar and singing, and wild monkeys were stealing food from neighboring rooftops. Of the many languages I detected, several were various accents of English, a few were tongues I recognized and a few I could not. I was one of the many international travelers that knocked on this door, which would be my home for a week. I filled my daypack, took a week's worth of mugger money, then discreetly stashed my money belt in a pile of crumbling cinder blocks and headed for the river.

Because the alleys are so narrow in this old town, there is no such thing as "street food," but I found a familiar yogurt shop that was just a cubbyhole too small to be able to stand in. From my perch on the pillows used for chairs I enjoyed the open view of the street. Inside this shoebox was a huge, boiling cauldron of steaming milk, and a tiny boy constantly stirred the copper kettle with a wooden paddle. I ordered up some of yesterday's yogurt, perfect in consistency and sprinkled with sugar, then settled in to people watch. Even with the absence of motorists, the street scene was lively. Merchants, shoppers, delivery carts and bicycles maintained a hectic pace. The yogurt merchant was purchasing milk from a bicycle delivery boy to feed today's cauldron. Young boys bargained for colorful kites, and nearby, a holy cow munched on garlands intended for the gods.

I made my way down to the river and walked its banks to inquire about renting a boat. A 12-year-old boy was bailing out his family's fleet of tourist boats. He introduced himself as Baboo, the Boatman. "My father is a boatman, his father is a boatman, I am a boatman," he boasted in his broken English. We talked for a while then I hired Baboo and his boat for the week.

As agreed, Baboo woke me the next day on the roof where I was staying. We began our three-hour voyage welcoming the day an hour before sunrise. I started off rowing upstream. The beautiful little tin boat sliced through the water swiftly but it leaked a bit. Before the first splinter of light, we rowed past the funeral fires burning on the ghats along the river's edge. At that time of the morning the primal silence of the river and the reflection from the fire made the tiny boat appear dreamlike.

The gods were stirring and the town was coming to life with chai salesmen, pilgrims, tourists and boatmen among its cast of characters. The morning air was chilly, but the water was warm enough for the morning bathers. A striking young girl rowed her little boat up to us. She was selling floating shrines made of leaves about the size of a teacup and decorated with garland. The candle in the middle was meant to be lit in prayers for your family and floated down river. I bought three of the little boat shrines for Baboo, the girl and myself. As we lit the candles and set them upon the current, Baboo and the girl bowed their heads in prayer while I quietly observed their reverence. A few feet away a pink river dolphin broke the surface to give its blessing to this special ritual.

Hours later I took Baboo to breakfast and he confided that he thought the flower girl was pretty. He thought out loud, "If I were to marry her, our son would be a boatman, too." Although he couldn't read or write, the waterfront was his school and the boat was his business. He promised to meet me again the next morning.

I left Baboo and wandered down the ghats to my favorite bhang lassi shop, where the locals practice yoga and massage. While I was busy surveying the hustlers, hawkers and phony guides, I noticed a friendly thin man with smiling eyes beckoning me to his side. He was dressed in an orange sarong and sat on a day bed in the shade of the trees. Two other pilgrims were sitting with him. I walked over for a bony handshake and sat at his feet to hear his story.

Dr. Gree was a dentist and the father of seven. At 70 he was too active for retirement and enjoyed meeting people, so he left his practice and the comforts of home and had spent the last year on the adventure of a pilgrimage. He had walked 1,200 miles north to reach this holy city. He had miraculously done this without shoes, shelter or money, totally relying on the grace of his nation. Now in Varanasi, Dr. Gree contented himself with hours of meditation, yoga, bathing and prayer all in preparation for passing into the next life. When I asked him what he had learned from his devotions, he said, "When I act from my highest good, my life flows better."

He talked of spiritual enlightenment and said every devout Hindu wants to visit Varanasi to purify body and soul in the river. It's believed that one drop of this holy river will give the seeker enlightenment. This means being in God's presence and looking forward to uniting with God, just as a drop of rain merges with the sea. Over the next six days Dr. Gree shared with me some of the amazing adventures from his 12-month pilgrimage. He told me that one's life is made up of an accumulation of small experiences. Dr. Gree spoke of Siddhartha, otherwise known as Buddha, whose teachings are the foundation of Buddhism. Siddhartha came to this very spot in Varanasi in 550 BC to deliver his first teachings.

Dr. Gree stopped eating altogether, and our sessions were getting shorter and shorter as the week continued. His eldest son had come to honor his father and help with the funeral arrangements. Dr. Gree told us he was rejoicing about the day his body would be burned and the sparks from his funeral pyre would set his soul free. His gentle heart warmed me inwardly.

The longer I stayed in India and studied this religion, the more fascinated I was by Hinduism. With hundreds of gods and goddesses that are worshipped daily, the Hindus are devout and possess an innocence of character. Everyday miracles are a part of these people's day-to-day lives, and because of their faith, it isn't extraordinary to them. It's who they are and what they believe in, and it is always in evidence at the river's edge. To transcend one's own boundaries and become more spiritually open and religiously tolerant – that's what India passes on to this traveler.

40

Pet Abuse

During my eight-month hitch around Australia, a tractor-trailer filled with grain picked me up outside a sleepy little town. It is commonplace for working-class Aussies to travel overseas for several years at a time, and my latest host, a burly middle-aged trucker named Jeff, talked about his own travels and odd jobs in Europe and coming home through Asia.

Jeff told me that in 1968, in a nearby dried-up lakebed called Mungo, 60,000-year-old human bones were found. As Australia is an island, the Mungo people must have crossed 60 miles or more of open water without knowing what lay ahead. Reaching Australia, they found their way over 2,000 miles inland from the north coast and settled on Lake Mungo. Before this find, anthropologists had no evidence or belief that *Homo sapiens* could even speak 60,000 years ago, let alone engage in a massive expedition, building seaworthy crafts and colonizing island continents! Jeff and I were in awe of anthropologist Jarod Diamond's book *Guns, Germs and Steel*, and his "two waves theory" on how humans dispersed across Euro-Asia. First *Homo erectus* and then *Homo sapiens* walked out of Africa 100,000 years ago. Jeff also shared with me that in the 1880s his grandfather helped build the Dingo Fence to protect flocks of sheep from predators in the southeastern farmland of Australia. This wire fence stretches 5,500 kilometers, making it one of the longest structures in the world.

In a sea of grain fields, we traveled until we came upon a small town just outside Melbourne. Deafening white cockatoos the size of chickens had descended in droves. In this grain-producing area the farms have huge concrete silos that attract clouds of birds. These vicious cockatoos have strong, razor beaks, which they occasionally sharpen by ripping the chrome and rubber off car windshields. They are very destructive! As we pulled into the granary to unload, a fellow trucker was extremely irate because of the damage the cockatoos had done to his windshield. With a sawed-off shotgun he was blowing away dozens of them out of trees in the picnic area. In the United States a cockatoo is a $1,000 pet, but in this farming community outside Melbourne they are bloody target practice, mate!

I was dropped off and began looking around for a ride going further south, which took awhile because of the crazy guy shooting cockatoos in the parking lot. My next goal was to get to the famous Mount Arapiles to go rock climbing. Even though Mount Arapiles was only a few hours away, it took me all the next day to get there through the remote western plains of Victoria. Arriving late in the day I set my tent up at the well-run free campground, which was nestled next to the pink sandstone cliffs. Arapiles is a popular climbing destination, and some people camp there for months at a time. I settled in for what would become a three-week stay. The cool weather, accessibility, quantity and quality of climbs, and a very chilled-out and beautiful camp scene have made Arapiles a world-class climbing destination.

I've always found the climbing community to be friendly, and here was no exception. It was a festive atmosphere of cooking, camping, mingling and partying. A couple of Melbourne weekenders purchased some of the silver bracelets I was selling and gave me their leftover food before leaving. I shared the bounty with my neighbors and struck up a conversation with a guy named Mitch. He was a lean, strong blonde who had a Dutch accent that was fun to hear. His parents were English missionaries, and Mitch had grown up on a tiny island in Dutch Indonesia. His nickname was "Little Frog" because he and a Chinese friend of his loved to climb coconut trees. Mitch was fluent in Mandarin, among many other languages.

In 1985, in his early 20s, Mitch went to China and began buying old jade and ivory. He learned that ivory turns a specific color when it is directly against a decomposing body. Buying these treasures off grave robbers and antiques dealers, Mitch smuggled them into Taiwan and sold them for a huge profit. On what became his final trip, he was arrested at the airport in China, thrown in jail without a trial and forgotten. His parents thought he was dead. Mitch grew his blonde hair into a long Chinese plait and wore a black Mao uniform. He was pale white from lack of sun and the superstitious Chinese called him "The Ghost." Being forever reverent of their ancestors, the Chinese were fearful of Mitch, which allowed him extra privileges. Three years after his incarceration Mitch was discovered by an Australian consulate, and it took another four years for his release. After his seven years of hell, Mitch was still worshipping his first year of freedom when we met, and his joy was rubbing off on everyone around him. That night we became friends and decided to be climbing partners.

The following morning, we grabbed our gear and set out for the orange cliffs. Being in the southern hemisphere it was sunny on the north side. Mount Arapiles is primarily composed of quartzite. The climbing there is one-and two-pitch sandstone routes and with names like "Pet Abuse," "Ethiopia," "Lord of the Rings," and "Slopin' Sleazin'," you know you're in for a serious adrenaline hit. We began our weeklong liaison on the classic routes. By week's end Mitch thought I was ready to lead the famous overhanging roof of Kachoong. This route is a heady hardcore undertaking. While not particularly high, this huge overhang is the epitome of man versus gravity. It was especially exhilarating because of the spectators who gather on the backside of the abutment towards the end of every Saturday to cheer on the warriors.

The start of Kachoong is in a damp corner. I headed up 70 vertical feet and placed a good piece of gear in the corner. Then came the freaky part, the horizontal traverse. At this point, I, like most climbers, was too gripped in fear to set any more protection. Jamming my knee, my foot and my hand deep in the crack, I horizontally left the wall, getting further, and further, and further from the ground and my protection. My critical mistake came when I couldn't get a feel for my next handhold, and with skinned knees and cramping fingers, I was gripped with panic! In my exhausted state of horizontal limbo, I tried desperately to ignore the peanut gallery of onlookers laughing and shouting catcalls.

Clearly I was not going to make it up and over the roof and when my feet fell out of the crack, I limply hung on. Before my hands finally surrendered, I screamed like a schoolgirl and took a 30-foot pendulum swing as the crowd went wild. The whipper into the wall hurt both my ego and my shoulder. Then I belayed for Mitch who seemed to effortlessly flash the famous Kachoong overhang with precision and grace. Still smarting from my bruising, I paid closer attention to Mitch's technique. When Mitch came down we joined the crowd below to the good-natured round of back slaps, roasted kangaroo legs and beer. Kachoong haunted me for the next two weeks. Mitch assured me I would "get it" before leaving Arapiles and eventually I did.

The crazy contrasts of this continent gave me pause to stop and ponder. There are the beefy truckers who don't give a second thought to blowing away beautiful birds, because after all, true Aussie cowboys have been battling the beasts of this harsh region for centuries. Then there is the more compassionate Australian climbing elite, who woo you with their intelligence and athletic prowess in harmony with nature. Being a man of unconventional adventures, I found it exhilarating to discover that tucked "Down Under" is an eclectic mix of spirit and soul.

New South Wales, Australia

41

Rustina on the Dempster

I was steering my present shitbox, a '74 Corolla that refused to die, in the direction of Alaska. With a spidery windshield and the peeling brown flakes of a hasty old paint job, it wasn't exactly a chick magnet. The AM radio had been my only companion on the endless stretch of the flat terrain of the Midwest. My Bondo Buggy made it to Wyoming, where I ditched her for a week to hike through Yellowstone, home of some of the most amazing trails and scenery in the world. In the late afternoon of the sixth day, I came across about a dozen eight-foot gravel circles next to a steaming thermal stream and for the life of me couldn't figure out what they were. What natural phenomenon caused this? I put up my tent in the center of the alien circle closest to the stream and tried to enjoy a dehydrated tuna-something from my pack while preparing to be abducted. I read a little bit by the light of my headlamp then fell asleep.

Sometime during the night I was suddenly awakened by a snort and shuffle of hooves. I nervously peeked out from inside my tent and, in the dark, could make out the silhouette of a herd of buffalo coming to lay up. It dawned on me that this was the reason for the gravel circles. The resourceful buffaloes made the rings to keep a layer of gravel between their bodies to avoid the dewy grass and the ticks. They shuffled all around and didn't seem perturbed by my presence as they lay down for the night: all except one. I hadn't escaped the attention of a massive bull buffalo, standing less than five feet away and eyeballing my camouflage tent warily. Hearing him paw the grass and listening to his snorts made me extremely uncomfortable. I was thinking that at any minute he was going to trample me in my tent. The buffalo was so close I could even smell his breath. Ten minutes later I peered out from a tiny opening and saw that the alpha leader had displaced a younger bull and was settling in for the night, still uncomfortably close.

Exhausted from hiking, somehow I managed to fall back to sleep. I always intend to break camp at dawn to avoid illegal camping fines. The sun was a pale pink on the horizon and, with the exception of the big alpha buffalo, the herd had moved on. Snorting and panting, he sounded like I felt. Desperate to get out of my tent, which was heating up like an oven, our stand-off continued for the better part of the morning until finally, around 10 o'clock, he got up and trailed into the mountain meadow. I broke down my intrusive campsite and headed for civilization to find a midmorning meal and cup of coffee.

It took quite awhile to hike back onto the main road, where I caught a ride. I was dropped off at the prestigious Old Faithful Inn where I had parked my car seven days earlier. This structure is the largest log hotel in the world and elegant in its proportions. Despite my roughshod appearance, I walked into the dining room and ordered the lovely cup of coffee I had been craving for days. Parked beside the huge 85-foot stone fireplace, I was admiring the many features of this national landmark, which included an attractive young woman clearing tables. She noticed my eyes sweeping the scenery and a few minutes later came over, pulled out the other chair at my table and sat down. "What's up, morning glory?" she said. "Hi-biscus," I replied.

And that was how I met Danielle, who went by Dani. She was a third-year student at Syracuse University in upstate New York, surviving on grants to finance her five-year plan. She had come west for a summer job. She loved hiking and the great outdoors, and Yellowstone was her new adventure. Dani got a job bussing tables at the inn for the summer, but on her off time she could most often be found camping. She confessed to being sick of the job. I told her about my buffalo confrontation of the night before, and she laughed. She asked where I was heading, and when I told her Alaska she plied me with a dozen questions. We chattered like a couple of blue jays

187

for the better part of an hour. This long-legged, rambunctious girl with closely cropped hair and sparkling green eyes enchanted me.

Dani's boss came over and reprimanded her for not working. She looked up at him, smiled sweetly and told him she was giving her five-minute notice because she was leaving for Alaska. I don't know who was more shocked, her boss or me! I was feeling pretty good about my new traveling partner in spite of the fact that she had not yet viewed the leaky chariot that would take us on our journey. She left to go gather her things, say goodbyes and returned thirty minutes later with her pack, a 20-pound wheel of sharp cheddar cheese that she borrowed from the kitchen, and a bottle of Windex. Dani asked if I was ready to go. I laughed and told her to toss her pack and cheese in "the bucket." She circled my heap twice as if inspecting it for purchase, then without a word threw her pack and the huge wheel of cheese on the backseat and jumped in the passenger side.

Dani's spontaneity, enthusiasm and hilarious company were a vast improvement to the AM radio, and we got along great as we headed northwest. We passed the miles by making up silly songs, and through the hot days and cool nights my rust bucket of a car held up admirably. Every time we got back into the car, this gorgeous young gal would sniff the air and say, "Papa, is that your feet?" referring to the huge, sweating wheel of cheese that was reeking in our rolling bedroom.

One afternoon while we were stopped for a herd of elk, I was assembling tomato, cheese and mustard sandwiches on the hood and noticed out of the corner of my eye that Dani was writing with my emergency hitchhiking marker on the back of the car. She saw me watching her over the roof of the car and broke into a long laugh, announcing, "Finally, she has a name. Come see what ya think." In capital letters across the entire expanse of the hatchback read: RUSTINA.

We stopped at almost every big bridge we came to for the relief it offered from the infinite forests that flanked the roads. Often we stopped just for the view of the raging, silty rivers and a few times used my climbing gear to rappel down to the edge of the river for a picnic. We had a break from our long road trip in the Klondike

Valley of Yukon, Canada. This spectacular setting is at the confluence of the Klondike and Yukon Rivers, and sitting on its edge is the old gold rush town of Dawson. We pulled into the parking lot of a tiny hole-in-the-wall bar and went in. Chicken wire was tacked up against the inside of the windows. This place looked as though it could get kind of rough, but the big weathered men that I took for the local loggers seemed friendly enough. At the bar I struck up a conversation with some nearby truckers to inquire about the famous Dempster Highway, which is Canada's only all-weather road going deep into the Arctic. The highway begins east of Dawson and extends 450 miles north to Inuvik all the way to the Beaufort Sea!

I found out that the design of the highway is unique, primarily due to the intense weather conditions of the area. The highway itself is a gravel berm designed to insulate the permafrost from the soil underneath. The thickness of the gravel pad ranges from four to seven feet. Without the pad, the road would literally sink into the ground in late spring. The trucker told me it was all about the grading and then asked me what kind of clearance I had on my truck. I casually told him I was planning to do it in my 20-year-old Corolla. He thought I was joking and laughed heartily.

Dani was playing pool with an enormous man called Tiny who offered to weld a skid plate on Rustina. The next day, true to his word, Tiny welded a heavy three-foot by five-foot steel plate to the undercarriage of Rustina, turning it into more of a sled-like vehicle that might be able to navigate the formidable Dempster Highway. Tiny told us another necessity would be spare tires, and he took care of that by helping us purchase four very cheap, very used ones that fit Rustina. We had no choice but to carry the tires on the roof and secured them to the rack with climbing rope. The heavy load of tires worsened Rustina's already leaky "custom" sunroof. Our spirits were high as we set out that afternoon with renewed supplies. We had gas, water, food, a new skid plate and five used tires. As an overlander, I had always wanted to drive the Dempster Highway, the most northern road in North America.

The single-lane gravel road of the Dempster is made up of shale and dirt. The massive mound in the middle was too high for

Rustina to clear. To avoid the mound created by truck traffic we had to straddle the rut and the shoulder, which left our tires exposed to being punctured by the sharp loose shale that had built up along the sides of the road. Now I understood the comment the trucker had made about grading and clearance being an essential component of passage on this crazy road. To make matters worse, if we encountered any obstacle that made it necessary to cross to the other side of the road, like a kicked-up boulder, Rustina trembled and shook violently. Her whole undercarriage was trying to be ripped out from under her as she attempted to clear the mound. Thank God for Tiny's skid plate!

After five deafening hours, only 90 miles and two flat tires, we pulled over as far as we could and set up our tent in front of Rustina. In this desolate, rolling tundra there wasn't a single, solitary sound when I turned off the engine, which magnified the eerie isolation Dani and I were both experiencing. Good judgment dictated that we turn around if we ever wanted Rustina to see tar again. Even though Dani was also rattled, we both laughed hysterically when the first vehicle to pass us since starting this insane journey was a huge gas truck. Its wheels very nearly hit our tent when it went by in the middle of the night.

The next full day we eked out a little over a hundred miles and blew two more tires. The reality of not making it had set in. We spotted a pickup truck parked on a tiny alcove off the road. We pulled up next to it and met the rifle-toting man who belonged with the truck. A middle-aged, gap-toothed Inuit named Charley Johnnie introduced himself in English, and we began to explain our dilemma. We were in immediate need of tires and gas. He tried to pay attention but it was fairly obvious he had his mind on something more pressing. He interrupted Dani to explain that he had a bit of an issue himself. He was out here hunting and had just spotted two caribou that had run up and over the hill nearby. He proposed that if we were willing to first help him herd the caribou back in his direction, he could at least help us get gas at a fair price. Dani and I did as Charley requested by walking 15 minutes in one direction, then hooking around back towards the truck. Underfoot, the thick, soft, spongy tundra was speckled with little red berries and fluorescent lime-green moss. As Dani and I crested over the last treeless knoll leading back to the vehicles, we heard three shots and upon return found our new friend leaning over two felled caribou.

Right there he proceeded to gut these tundra beasts and cut them in half using a bow saw. We helped him load the steaming carcasses on a child's orange plastic sled but could only muscle one portion of a caribou to the road at a time. Using a couple of planks we helped him drag the bloody remains into the bed of his truck. We were all tired and filthy from the effort. Charley followed us into Eagle's Plain, the one location to stop for food and fuel along the entire distance of this isolated region.

Charley was extremely grateful for our efforts and graciously invited us for the night into his tiny home on the edge of town. We welcomed the opportunity to shower and then settled in for a big caribou stew prepared by his wife and children. Dani and I spent a comfortable evening with this warm native family and were able to laugh at ourselves while our host told goodnatured jokes about our wacky adventure in little Rustina.

Given the sad state Rustina was in, we had to take stock of the situation and reassess our game plan. Gas was no longer a problem, but Charley could get his hands only on one extra tire. He told us the town of Inuvik was our only option for extra tires. Clearly Rustina was not going to make the last 250 miles. Dani and I decided we could make it by hitchhiking and find the extra tires we needed to get Rustina back down the Dempster the way we had come. Our trusty rust bucket was in good hands parked at Charley's house, so we set off the next day with three rims and our backpacks. My adventure partner had never hitched, before and I marveled that her first experience was on one of the most inaccessible segments of road in the world!

We waited at the intersection a good hour for the first truck going north. Dani flailed and waved her arms in the middle of the road to ensure that the truck had to stop, or kill her. The driver took in her request, her gear and her guy and resolutely told her, "No way." We waited about another hour for the next Dempster travelers and were finally rewarded with a white pickup whose cab was already full of locals. This time she didn't wait for an answer and we were loading our rims, bodies and packs in the back before the bewildered natives knew what had hit them. The rugged sidewalls on their tires said that the residents of this area understood the necessity of proper equipment. Riding trucks was old hat for me and it has never lost its appeal. However, Dani had never stood up in the bed of a truck while whipping down the road. The sunshine paled in comparison to her crackling energy, radiant smile and fresh hair. Her scent lingers with me still.

Dani on the Dempster

42
Skull Juggling

It seems like I am a magnet for bizarre situations! On my fifth month of touring through West Africa in 2002, I found out that the real show in Mali is not Timbuktu, but a cluster of villages preserving traditional rituals and belief systems. This area is called the Dogon. In the capital of Bamako I met a German traveler named Hans. We were both considering a tour of the ancient sandstone cliffs, another UNESCO World Heritage Site. After a couple of beers and swapping some adventure stories, we decided that real men don't take tours; we would do it on our own.

The next day Hans and I hitched to the Dogon, where we met a nice Muslim family who lived in a mud house on the edge of a small village. Unlike most of their neighbors, their two-room house had a flat roof made of timber, straw and mud, from on top of which we had the best view of the Bandiagara Cliffs. For a small sum they agreed to let us put up my tent on a section of the roof. The only rule was we were to steer clear of the rotten half of roof covered in plastic.

One thousand years ago, pygmies carved two miles of dwellings into the vertical Bandiagara Cliffs, consisting of stacked buildings, caves and tombs that are accessible only by ladders. The tiny pygmies lived in this unusual structure to hide from the Muslim kingdom of the north and later from the French. Sadly, they were discovered and had to flee to the Congo just a few hundred years ago. These magical abandoned cliffs remain the focal point of the Dogon area. Today, the Dogon's tall proud culture practices its own mythology with mask dances and wooden sculptures and features very unique architecture.

A tour guide said it was illegal to climb the cliffs, but later we found out that the locals do it, so Hans and I ignored the rules and decided to forge our own path. At dawn the next day we jumped the fence that was intended to keep out trespassers and headed for the pale, rose-colored cliffs. The multitude of ladders was well protected from the annual rainfall by the overhanging rock. Made from trees hundreds of years ago, each log ladder was roughly 15 feet tall. The stairs were trees on angle with notched-out steps. It was easy to get high and deep into this vertical city using the hundreds of ladder stairs.

It was awe-inspiring to be in the catacomb cliff dwellings littered with pottery, which was evidence of a past civilization. Hans and I sat on a stone balcony with our feet dangling out over a few hundred feet, mesmerized by the plains before us. We could make out the activity of the village below and marveled at the tight cluster of small homes made of pink sandstone block, topped with thatched, cone-style roofs.

Hans and I wore headlamps to explore the recessed caves and entered a room that had huge clay urns filled with nothing but skulls. What did they do with the rest of the body? How many people lived here? Wandering freely through these ruins made me feel more alive, but not having a guide we had to accept the mystery of our surroundings. We'd have to ask our questions when we got back to the city. Ignorance is bliss, they say, but lack of respect is not. I began juggling three pygmy skulls to the delight of Hans, who was filming me. Even more disrespectfully, I took a small bit of fabric and pottery and put it in my pocket. In my world I know that karma is a bitch with a whip, and this ancient site would soon have its revenge.

I was leading the way up a log ladder when I looked behind me and saw Hans's grimacing face. I followed his gaze and looked up to see a dark cloud descending. It took a few seconds to register that the hum accompanying this black shadow was an enormous swarm of bees. They were pouring out of a crack in a large grave urn full of skulls – thousands of them! Months earlier in this trip I had been warned about the killer/honey bee hybrid, and now they were landing on me everywhere! These small bees were in my eyes and up

194

my nose. I didn't dare open my mouth. As a house painter I'd been stung quite a few times, but I'd never seen or felt anything like this in my life. There I was, 200 feet above the ground, with dozens of bees landing all over me, and thousands more swarming around my head. I knew I had to bid a hasty retreat and began climbing carefully down the ladder. I sucked one bee up my nose and into my throat. It stung the back of my mouth before I could cough it out. I was really starting to freak out. I mistakenly rubbed my face and killed a dozen bees in the process. The signal was out: sting this bastard to death! When dozens of bee stingers hit their mark, I threw caution to the wind and began to run down the ladders.

I ran right past Hans, thinking that if I could just get to the ground, maybe I could outrun the swarm. My eyes and throat were swelling shut. Waving my hands frantically trying to clear my vision of these angry bastards, I picked the most direct ladder system to the ground. I didn't take the time to test the strength of the steps before applying my weight, and halfway down an ancient log ladder broke in half. I fell at least 10 feet and landed on my hands and knees on a dusty stone floor. Unfortunately my forehead broke the momentum. With a deep cut over my right eye, my vision was nearly gone as I continued to run down the remaining ladders to the ground. By this time, I was completely hysterical, windmilling my arms, running and screaming into the open desert. I ran as fast as I could. After about a quarter of a mile, I noticed that while the bees that had made their way into my hair, sinus cavities and clothing remained, the swarm was gone. I spit out the last bees with what breath I had left and threw up the ones I had inhaled, then waited for Hans to see if he had been attacked as badly.

He was following slowly behind me, and I was astonished to find out he hadn't been stung. Not even once! Later, picking stingers out of me with my Swiss army knife tweezers, Hans estimated I had taken fifty or so stings. My eyes were swollen shut, my lips were three times their normal size and my cheeks had huge welts. I looked like a pumpkin. Hans got me up to the tent on the roof and nervously asked me what I needed. "Beer," I whimpered. To make my karma worse, Hans bribed the Muslim daughter to go to the

Chinese shop in order to buy the contraband. I drank four liters of foreign extra stout with rusty caps until I was D-R-U-N-K, drunk.

This is the crazy part. I was so drunk and so blind that when I went to take a piss around sunset, I thought I was aiming off the side of the house, but actually pissed on the plastic roof of our hosts' bedroom - the forbidden zone. Hans quickly scolded me; I turned, slipped on the wet plastic and belly-flopped through the very rotten roof, taking all the plastic with me. My shin was painfully smashed as I half-landed on the family bed. Thank God the family was preparing dinner in the next room. I rolled over in a daze, pants down to my knees, and looked up at the stars through the huge hole I'd just created in the roof. Through the sliver of vision in my good eye I could just make out Hans staring down in horror. Our host and his wife were understandably irate and began screaming at me in French. Hans quickly saved the day by pulling up my pants, removing my money belt and giving our host more than enough money to fix the entire roof, while apologizing profusely for his stupid friend. How did this wonderful day turn into such a shit show?

As we were leaving the next day, I made sure I left behind the pottery shards and fabric that were in my pocket to hopefully appease the gods. I felt like I'd been hit by a truck. I could barely see out of my left eye, and my purple right eye was closed shut with a large open gash on my eyebrow. I knew I looked terrible. I limped blindly down the road with Hans leading the way. It seemed everybody we met already knew the story and delighted in laughing at the stupid ugly tourist. We stayed in town, where I hid in a cheap hotel room.

In the absence of TV, I was prime-time entertainment for this small town. Despite the lack of modern technology, news travels very fast in this part of the world. After taking the bus to another small town an hour and a half away, a few characters imitated me in a public place by pretending to violently wave bees off themselves and scream like a girl, to the delight of the people around them. The entire town already knew the story and had lined up to get a look and a laugh. I had to ride another four hours to the capital city to heal in peace and obscurity.

A week later I still sported a very bruised ego, but I looked fairly normal except for the gash over my eye and the matching one on my shin. I continued my trip alone but learned two valuable lessons: be respectful, and if you really mess up, take a long, long bus ride.

Dogon Mask Dance, Mali, West Africa

43
Egypt

You can call me insensitive, but I prefer to visit an area after a terrorist attack or natural disaster simply for its lack of tourists. That's how much I hate crowds. In November 1997, Muslim terrorists armed with automatic weapons ambushed, shot and killed 62 tourists at the Luxor temples in Egypt. All the gunmen were shot dead or immediately apprehended by military police. The Egyptian government denounced this act and quickly tightened security in and around major tourist centers. I changed my Asian plans for the following year and instead headed for the Middle East.

In 1998 I was one of a dozen independent travelers in the Valley of the Queens. Normally, by 10:00 in the morning there would be 30 idling buses in the parking lot. I walked down the ancient stone stairs of a famous large tomb, my headlamp lighting the way. A well-spoken, well-dressed guide met me in the burial chamber. He asked me the standard dozen questions – what was my good name? Where was I from? Blah, blah, blah. Then he said something very unique, something I had never heard from a guide before. "If I show you something amazing, truly amazing," he asked, "will you give me a five-dollar tip?" "Brother," I replied, "it's gotta be just shy of the Holy Grail as I live on only 15 dollars a day."

The guide lit a second candle and asked me to turn my headlamp off. He started with his standard tour of his interpretations of the hieroglyphics, and his theories of a culture about which little is known. We had the place all to ourselves! After 20 minutes of exploring the carved Egyptian glyphs, he went to the corner where giant urns are stored in the burgled tomb. The thick terracotta urns are about four feet tall and rest on a point. Here, he told me, an Egyptian queen had been buried with her servants, oil, wine, dates, nuts, and honey, and plenty of gold for the afterlife. I was starting to cringe. Unless he was about to pull a rabbit out of his ass, there was no way he was getting a five-dollar tip.

He picked up the bottom of a broken urn about the size of a grapefruit, blew off the cobwebs, cleaned the inside with his shirt, and with a big smile touched his tongue to the inside of it. In the flickering light he passed it to me and I licked it, too. Wow, 3,000-year-old honey, the perfect food. I happily passed him a five and we parted the best of friends.

Our funny guide, Egypt

44
Thousand-Dollar Rubber Band

The painkillers are making everything seem like a dream. My dry tongue is checking out my new dental crown, which seems a little too big for my mouth. I am desperate for water. I am in the intensive care unit of one of the best children's hospitals in India. It seems to be entirely Muslim. After 20 years I finally did it. I have just had a hemorrhoidectomy and three days ago received a dental bridge and crown.

The hospital is in Hyderabad, an ancient, colorful and friendly Muslim city with great food, beautiful mosques and crazy traffic. My famous pediatric doctor has a ZZ Top beard, giraffe eyes and a great sense of humor. He tries to schedule his medical practice around the five calls to prayer a day. I never saw my dentist's face as she was wearing either a surgical mask or a full Muslim hijab. Both my doctor and dentist spoke fluent English, and they, and almost everything around them, worked with perfect professionalism. This week I have spent $1,000. This amount included surgery, one night in intensive care, two nights in a beautiful private hospital room, medication, full blood work, a bridge and a crown, five new pairs of prescription eyeglasses, food, taxi fare and hotel accommodations for a week. A true half-century tune-up. India, I love you!

I watch the clock on the wall; 15 more minutes before my Florence Nightingale lets me drink. I am drier than a popcorn fart, and my swollen tongue is stuck to the roof of my mouth. I'm delighted that I get to see the head nurse's face as she takes my blood pressure and injects something into the port in my hand. She is one of the few women in Hyderapad not in purdah, the complete covering from head to toe that most Muslim women wear in public in this conservative city. The beeping of everyone's monitors adds to my dreamlike state.

Twenty years ago my sister introduced me to a colleague of hers, a doctor in Maine. At the time I was a rock climbing guide and taught teenagers about camping, climbing and life during their summer vacations. The doctor and I struck a deal over the telephone to barter a simple banding of my hemorrhoids in exchange for a guided father/son rock climbing adventure. He was totally up for it and seemed like a great guy. At his private office the next week I dropped my pants for the procedure. The doctor and his supermodel nurse Barbie started laughing unprofessionally as they viewed my hemorrhoids. He cried "Oh, my god!" while she suppressed her laughter. This, of course, did not help my self-esteem. I could have punched them both. Dr. Chucklehead rubbed numbing gel onto my hemorrhoids, but did not even wait long enough for the gel to take effect, and quickly banded just the largest one of the four. The doctor pushed the hemorrhoids back up in, popped his gloves off, and still laughing, scribbled out a prescription and sent me on my way. This could not have taken more than five minutes from the time I dropped my drawers to the time I rebuckled my belt.

Walking painfully, I reached for the door handle when the sour middle-aged receptionist stood up quickly and barked, "Where are you going? You've not paid your bill yet!" The giggling in the other room suddenly stopped as I introduced myself and explained the barter arrangement. Still standing, the secretary handed me a bill for $1,000 and announced that they "did not take credit". I reintroduced myself and tried to tell her again about the arrangement, as Dr. Chucklehead nervously came out and agreed with her, then quickly scurried away. Then the receptionist said, "Let me introduce myself, I am the doctor's wife and I take care of all of the billings. If you don't have the money with you, leave your driver's license and go get it." What could I do? They were acquaintances of my sister.

The $1,000-dollar rubber band was still burning my ass as I counted out ten $100 bills on the desk and demanded a receipt. I was furious. Anger turned to guilt a month later when I found out the doctor's son had shot himself in the head by the duck pond behind their home. Rich or poor, for $100 or for free, all the teenagers who went rock climbing with me grew an inch in a day in self-confidence; I should have gone rock climbing with that kid.

10-Day Adventure Course: Hitchhiking, Camping, & Rock Climbing

45
Pakistan

A day into Pakistan I was still shit scared. Pakistan? I can't believe I'm here. The media projected this place as being full of religious fanatics supporting Al-Qaeda. Lahore was a sizeable enough city that I needed a cab to get to the northern bus station. The friendly cabbie was exactly my age. We had a strange conversation through his rear view mirror. He wanted to know how many girlfriends I had and how much money I made. My Muslim driver had six children and said he had never seen his wife naked in their 25 years of marriage. He found my bus, introduced me to the driver, and insisted on carrying my pack to the closest tea shop. He bought tea for us out of the tip money I'd given him.

A sad young boy brought water in dirty chipped cups to my new friend and me. The boy's T-shirt was torn, dirty and clearly way too small for him. He pointed to the corner of the café under the stairs and told me he slept there. The adjacent kitchen was a mess from the night before, and I decided against eating there. Instead, I shared some candy with the boy. He looked so old and tired for one so young. We heard the call to prayer, and the restaurant emptied.

I walked across the street and started talking to the luggage boy while he strategically loaded the top of our bus, which was about to leave for the northern Karakorum region. Half an hour later, high on their prayers, the men returned, and the cabbie passed my pack up to the luggage boy. My friend the cabbie told me to sit on the right-hand side in order to be able to see the raging river we would soon be passing. I bought a bag of cut mango, papaya and watermelon through my half-opened dirty window. The dew sparkled in the morning with the late rising sun, and the smell of autumn was in the air. I looked forward to riding the roof in a few hours when the day warmed up.

First to get on the bus was a fat man who sported a large gold watch and a hajji, the white-laced cap that shows one has made the pilgrimage to Mecca. There was a large circular callus on his forehead from repeatedly touching his head to the ground in prayer. Next to board was an old man. Toothlessly, he smiled at me. "As-salamu alaykum (peace be upon you)," I greeted him. His face lit up even more as he gave the traditional response, "Wa alaykumu s-salam (upon you be peace)." The fat man abruptly turned around and skeptically asked me if I was Muslim. "Allah is in everyone's world," I replied and offered both men some fruit. The adorable old man accepted a piece of watermelon and sucked it merrily, clearly excited by the journey ahead. A small transistor radio was tied round his neck with shoestring, and he listened endlessly to unintelligible Muslim chanting. He told me that the best songs are the songs to God. Traditionally the first three rows of every bus in Pakistan are saved for women. A young woman in purdah got on with a small child. I checked out the only parts of her body that were visible, her hands and her ankles. I wondered what kind of woman she would look like without all that getup. I was still trying to make sense of this male-dominated, friendly country through my narrow Western frame of reality.

The remaining cast of characters was slowly filling the bus. A middle-aged man in a crisp white shirt and blue blazer sat down beside me and introduced himself as Muhammad. He was a poor country doctor, had studied years ago in the city of Lahore, and was on his way back from a class reunion. Most of his colleagues had since moved to England, Canada or the U.S. He told me he was content with his decision to stay and work in Pakistan, and that I was in for a spectacular ride. I found him to be soft in his religion, surprisingly open minded and a great conversationalist. He accepted my explanation that I wasn't too keen on organized religion and that my idea of God was personal. We talked of crazy King George Bush and how my president was affecting the world. Muhammad said his life had been very full. His first wife, Fatima, was his college sweetheart and the love of his life. She had given him two beautiful daughters, the oldest one now living in Canada. He had recently married a second wife, a widow with two kids; it sounded like it was his first wife's idea. "Men view their life through their achievements, while women view their life through their relationships," he said. They all lived in a small house, and his first wife enjoyed having kids around again. I guess he thought it had just been the right thing to do at the time. Muhammad said, "Where we're going, the mountain farmers are poor, but rich in family and spirituality. Most of my patients can't pay me in full, but I own my house, and there is food on the table." Together in silence we watched the river unfold through the massive mountains. At one point I jumped off the bus to help the luggage boy haul a dozen hobbled goats up the back ladder onto the bus roof and tie them down. The day was starting to warm up and I stayed on the roof. I was comfortably tucked behind the heap of luggage with a perfect view of the goats, the Himalayas and a raging river. The farmers we passed returned my waves. I realized my fear had gone and I was beginning to love this country.

Weeks later I was in the Himalayan region of the Pakistan-China border. Marco, a wild Australian, had picked me up six days earlier with his old BMW motorcycle, and I was riding on his luggage rack, towering a full foot above his head. He was an overlander coming from Germany on his way back to Australia. This guy was a true road warrior, looking like something out of a *Mad Max* movie with his well-worn leathers and crazy blonde hair. People told us that the Karakorum Pass into China was closed for the season but we wanted to check it out for ourselves.

The giant Himalayan mountains were still shadowing the road at 11:00 am. Marco was driving only 30 miles an hour on the icy road. You know how things appear to happen in slow motion right before you crash? That's what it was like when suddenly the front end fell away and the bike was going down. In slow motion I heard the last of my air forming the word "fuuuuuck" as I watched my sandals and black socks pass Marco's helmet. Tuck in your head and land on your pack, I thought to myself. As I skidded down the road, I rolled hard on my shoulder and smashed the left side of my helmetless head. Shaking off the stars, I looked up to see my friend trying to right his massive motorcycle. I slowly got to my feet and with a victory cry of survival that echoed off the mountains, I hobbled over to help Marco. His piercing blue eyes were wide with shock as he said, "Turning around is still moving forward," and we slowly headed back to the border of India.

Marco and local friends, Pakistan

46
Middle of Nowhere, Zimbabwe

I picked the least rusty can of beans from a dusty shelf and found a shady tree, sat on my pack and opened the can with a Swiss army knife. An old man with a large bundle on his head was coming into view. He slowed, left the road, and joined me. Thoughts of botulism, bachelorism and flatulence came to mind as the last of the congealed globs slid down my gullet. Shyly, the old man asked if he could have the can. I watched him wiggle the lid back and forth until it broke free. He licked the top clean and slid it into a crease in his tribal wrap. He poured a bit of water into the can, then with a finger swished it around and drank the dregs. He then pinched the can between his car tire sandals, and with a rock he tapped out a rhythmic beat on it to bend the jagged edges. He looked up with a huge smile, showing the gap in his teeth. He'd had the courage to ask a white traveler for his empty can, and now he had a drinking cup. What a day! As we beamed at each other, I thought to myself that this man must live on less than a dollar a day. Talk about treading lightly on the planet.

He watched me write my next cardboard destination, walk off down the road and start to hitch. Two hours of walking down that sleepy road put me in the middle of nowhere, Zimbabwe. After a dozen vehicles passed by, a tired old truck pulled over. The trucker got out without looking at me, went to the ditch and urinated. He shook himself dry then turned to shake my hand. He was power tripping, and I wasn't surprised when he demanded a price that was higher than the bus fare. After some very heated bargaining I paid him, climbed in the shaded cab and he instantly became friendly. This was how they do things in Africa. Game on!

It was a blue '56 Bedford, too worn for its original engine with most of the paint gone and a new wooden cargo body. The interior was vintage in a Spartan way. It had no trucker's adornments like in the rest of the world. The only thing holding the passenger door closed was a tiny rusty latch and the window seemed to be permanently down. With no radio, the flap, flap, flap of the separating retreads was our day`s constant melody. This 10-wheeler was loaded to the gills and its top speed was 30 miles an hour. Not having paid for their ride, the boys on the roof were not welcome into the luxury of our shaded cab. It was hotter than hell out there.

Tendai, as he was called, had short tufts of salt-and-pepper hair and a cream shirt stretched tight around his barrel chest, every button straining with pressure. His black wash 'n' wear trousers were rolled up to show his Chinese sandals dancing as he double-clutched the old truck while his big hands tamed the unruly steering wheel. His eyes were bloodshot and his pupils were clouded by cataracts. He had a patchy week's worth of growth on his jaw, a huge bulbous nose, a thick neck, and sour breath. His teeth, however, were perfectly white, and boy, did Tendai love to smile. I'm sure making a couple of extra bucks from me helped.

Tendai invited me to stay with his family on his day off. He spent most of the day lounging in his hammock in the shade while being doted on by his wife and many kids. I didn't blame him, I mean, he was doing nothing at home, but six days a week he never left that bouncing sweatbox, driving by day, sleeping in it by night. It was a tough way to make a living. I went downtown to buy some beers for us and sweets for the kids. In this big black township, I was the only white guy. When I mentioned I was Tendai's friend, people couldn't do enough for me. Tendai's face lit up when I brought him back the beer.

On our third day together, I asked Tendai what he would do if he had plenty of money. He just shrugged. Every two hours I bugged him with the same question. That night, pitching my tent in front of his truck, I pretended to threaten him, "If you don't give me an answer to that question, I'm hitching another truck tomorrow." But these questions were as alien as I was. He was African, a man of the moment, and he couldn't think further than his next meal. So, over a cup of weak coffee and porridge the next day, my friend surprised me as he blurted out, "Eat meat, drink beer, and have sex. Yeah, plenty of sex." We both roared with laughter. Some things are universal.

Hot, slow and dusty. Africa

47
Crazy Christmas Mornings

It had been a crazy few years of travel. The last three Christmases had found me in Guatemala, India and Egypt. In 1985, exactly two years ago this Christmas morning, my traveling companion Mark and I were driving south from Belize into Guatemala. At 10:30 in the morning I was eating some chocolate, having a smoke and reading my girlfriend Elizabeth's Christmas card for the second time, when Mark, who doesn't swear or smoke, swore loudly as he popped out the Led Zeppelin tape, rolled up the windows and ordered me to "put that fucking thing out." My warm daydream was shattered as I turned and looked into a tank turret pointed at our windshield! The turret swiveled to follow our hippie van into a large military checkpoint. Holy shit, welcome to Guatemala's civil war!

A stern officer ordered us to pull over and follow him into his nearby office for inspection of our paperwork. After showing our passports and the van's registration, we were told a search of our van was to be conducted. We returned to the reeking van where I had absentmindedly locked the keys inside. I nervously went up on the roof of the van and tried to pop the door lock from the open sunroof. The officer in charge followed me up onto the roof and pointed his automatic rifle at me. The first thought in my paranoid mind was he is going to shoot me in the back! Instead, with his polished boot he slid me aside and lay down next to me. Putting his head into the reeking van the officer effortlessly popped the lock with his rifle's gun sight.

When Mark opened the door, I raised my arms up in aggressive optimism, and the brigade of Mayan teenage soldiers gave out a loud victory cheer. Our serious officer gave up a little smile and it seemed like this might go better than expected. Mark immediately proceeded to hand out a carton of cheap Mexican cigarettes and a case of matches to the troops. Leaving the van door open to air out my morning illegal smoke, Mark climbed up and joined us on the roof. What a bizarre sight: watching 200 young Mayan soldiers in oversized American military uniforms, clouds of cheap Mexican tobacco smoke, with the turret of the tank still pointed directly at us. Christmas mornings don't get any weirder than that!

Moving an hour down the road that same afternoon to the amazing Mayan ruins of Tikal, we met up with a dozen international travelers. We all enjoyed a spectacular sunset on Temple Number Five amongst the ruins, toucans and howler monkeys. We bribed the guard with Christmas food and drink and he let us sleep up on top of the Mayan pyramid, high above the jungle canopy.

The following year's Christmas was also very strange. Mark and I were in Varanasi, India for the first time. Varanasi is the holiest Hindu center and oldest living city in the world. I was rowing in the predawn mist of the Ganges River feeling like more of a ghost than a person after our bhang lassis. While watching the flames of a blazing funeral pyre on shore, Mark and I caught sight of a vulture eating the remains of a corpse on the opposite bank. In the predawn light pilgrims were just beginning to pray and bathe in the holy water of the Ganges.

On the following Christmas Eve, Mark and I watched an amazing sunset on Mount Sinai in Egypt. It was below freezing and started to snow. All we had for the night were our three-season sleeping bags. Miraculously a toothless old candy salesman appeared out of nowhere. He opened a stone shed, lit a blazing fire inside the open doorway and invited us to stay for the night. We literally had to jump over the fire to get into the stone shed. As a Christmas present Mark and I paid double the asking price for our new friend's entire box of candy and then proceeded to eat it with him. The three of us gorged on delicious chocolate and were toasty warm as it snowed throughout the night. We woke up to two inches of snow on Mount Sinai. Sunrise on the 7,497-foot summit was phenomenal. The contrast of pure white snow on dark brown desert hills as far as the eye can see with 1,500-year-old Saint Catherine's Monastery in the background is staggering. I couldn't believe it; I was making a snowman in Africa on the top of Mount Sinai where Moses found the stone tablets of the Ten Commandments after leading his people out of slavery! What will next Christmas bring? God only knows.

Good planets are hard to find.

48
The Present Is the Present

The only facts I remember from Psych 101 are that women talk a whole lot more than men, the average person thinks 50,000 thoughts per day, and a mere 60 of those thoughts for men are sexual. Fifty thousand seemed astronomically high, while 60 seemed extremely low.

It was in Nepal that I rediscovered how extremely beneficial it is to be able to quiet the mind. That summer and fall I had hung out with a girl named Julie. We really enjoyed each other's company and as a painter, my days off are when it rains and in New England, that is often. It allowed us plenty of time for hitchhiking, canoeing and camping trips together. She was really special and I was missing her before I even left.

Our last week together was hard on us. I was leaving and she was being left. While she drove me to the airport, my last 10 minutes with her were a living hell. Her feelings of abandonment raged forth as she drove. Her young, beautiful face had become distorted with hatred and anger. "You are so shallow, you bigshot traveler. You are only good at running from reality. You hypocrite! You and your rose-colored glasses living in your beautiful bubble; you say live for the moment. Yet you are afraid of commitment and reality. Now that summer is gone you are done with me and are running from the cold weather. You are an aggressively optimistic cream sucker, and I never want to see your phony ass again! I am looking for an educated man with a real job, one who is looking towards the future, someone who will be there for me." She had timed it perfectly as we pulled up to the Delta Airlines departure. Gutted, I grabbed my pack, got out and shut the door. I bent over to look through the window into her wet, raging green eyes. She paused, and then finished me off, "You are going to die unhappy and alone, Peter Pan." She drove off and was gone. Wow! Everything she said seemed to hold some truth. My first-class flight to Paris sucked. The champagne was too sweet and the weather was cloudy. My mood was shitty. Even the first week in India was getting on my nerves. I had let her steal my mojo.

I must have rewound that 10-minute monologue five thousand times, and all the beautiful summer memories we shared slowly faded. It just kept popping up in my head every waking hour. The negative thoughts were sabotaging my happiness and this trip. While I was traveling with a 50-year-old Dutchman for a week, he strongly recommended a 10-day silent meditation course in Nepal called Vipassana.

The next month found me silently sitting in the dark with my eyes closed and focusing only on reality. We were told that our thoughts, like dreams, are not real, should not be allowed to harm us and to pay little attention to them. For 10 days, every waking hour I focused on my breath, flesh, and aching back. As a thought would interrupt my meditation I would simply let it go. I was discovering an amazing thing: the less attention I paid to negative thoughts, the less they came back.

On day five I had a breakthrough. I could feel my entire body, both inside and out, and my chaotic mind was clear for the first time in my life! The true power in my life is me the thinker and not my thoughts. I am the producer and editor of my positive mind. I have more awareness now to slow down, quiet my mind and filter out negative thoughts. My higher self awakened, and this newfound wisdom came with intuition and creativity. Yes, aggressive optimism had returned. Intuition gave me the wisdom to want and attempt to get closer to some people while avoiding others. It gave me the ability to make quick, accurate decisions without a map or the local language skills.

Day after day I followed an invisible energy, which guided me in the right direction. The simplicity of following the sun with little food and money, a tent and intuition allows me to move around the world safely. Aggressive optimism shields me from daily negative situations and protects me with the aura of a positive mindset. It also allows for a higher threshold for discomfort.

I was lucky to grow up in a rural part of the country with doors that were never locked and a large, loving family. I was taught that strangers could be kind and good things happened to people who did good deeds. Meditation allows that regression back to childhood innocence, which seems the natural way of living in the moment without analyzing or keeping score. I thrive on the adventures of a new day. This optimistic courage, combined with the acceptance of not knowing, is my personal Magical Mystery Tour. The more I smile and love on people, the more they smile and love in return.

My life is greatly improved by paying attention to how I am living and less upon how I am doing. It goes hand in hand with the old lesson of "it's not getting what you want; it's wanting what you have." Being mindful of the little things such as children playing or the leaves falling in a forest, the sound of a stream or the smile of a passing stranger are simple things that can be the highlights of some days. When I calm my mind, I am not disturbed by small problems and am free to live a full life. I've learned that negative thoughts create fears. I want to be happy, do my best and have fun.

Now that you are close to the end of this book I ask you, the reader, if this simple philosophy could also increase your courage to be happier? I was taught by meditation that our past is a figment of our imagination and our future will come soon enough. We only have one short life to live. The present is the present!

49

Shine On!

Our deepest fear is not that we are inadequate.
Our deepest fear is that we are powerful beyond measure.
It is our light, not our darkness that most frightens us.
We ask ourselves, who am I to be brilliant, gorgeous, talented, fabulous?
Actually who are you not to be?
You are a child of God.
Your playing small doesn't serve the world.
There is nothing elegant about shrinking so that other people won't feel insecure around you.
We are all meant to shine, as children do.
We were born to make manifest the glory of God that is within us.
It's not just in some of us; it's in everyone.
And as we let our light shine,
we unconsciously give other people permission to do the same.
As we are liberated from our own fear,
our presence automatically liberates others.

-Marianne Williamson

July 22, 2009, like every day that month, dawned dark and foggy. In spite of the weather we pulled anchor and finally we were on our way north. Our captain Ollie at 25 years old was exactly half my age and owned a 30-foot Akin cutter. The *Alyssa* is a spectacular wooden sailboat. This polished classic beauty is a real supermodel.

Along with Ollie, 19-year-old Leif and I rounded out the crew. Leif had just finished his schooling in boat systems in Maine and was like a sponge, absorbing everything regarding sailing. After leaving us Leif was going to help an older couple sail around the world in a 60-foot Swan. He was quiet, clever and rugged, with a well-developed sense of humor, and it was a delight to have him on board.

Ollie was a friend of two of my nieces, Courtney and Marit, and I had watched the three of them grow up together. We had been on numerous climbing, hiking and canoeing trips with the occasional city field trip. They had all turned out to be solid adults. I was quite proud of them and enjoyed their company. Ollie had just retired from bicycle racing in Europe. He had graduated from Maine Maritime Academy and was pursuing his next passion as a captain. Ollie helped run tugboats from Washington to Alaska up the Inner Passage for a year to save money to buy the *Alyssa*. I was the old guy on the trip and would witness the transformation of these two men from travelers to full-on explorers, learning quite a bit myself in the process.

In Maine on that misty morning we stepped onto the boat ready to set sail. Each of us had our own goal for the trip. Ollie wanted to sail his boat to St. John's, Newfoundland. Twelve hundred miles east of New York City, it is the farthest point east in North America. Leif brought his surfboard and wanted to catch big waves in the cold Atlantic waters. As for me, I had hitched around Newfoundland a half dozen times and had become obsessed with icebergs. I brought ice-climbing gear with the goal of sailing up to an iceberg to climb it.

We sailed 66 hours well off the coast to our first port of call, Lunenburg, Nova Scotia. This harbor is known as the wooden boat capital of Canada and the home of the *Bluenose*, the beautiful schooner embossed on the Canadian dime. We cleared customs on a rainy Sunday night by VHF radio, successfully smuggling in a dozen duty-free gallons of rum.

The sun finally decided to show her face and cast her glow on the picturesque hamlet of Lunenburg harbor, where we rested up after having sailed for three days through pea-soup fog and drizzling rain. We felt rejuvenated and invited a few new friends and neighbors aboard the *Alyssa* for an impromptu party. Among them were a couple anchored next to us who had just sailed around the world miraculously without an engine, a young passing kayaker, and three waitresses we had met in town at breakfast. These girls were fishermen's daughters and knew how to handle a dory and a mixed drink. With our new friends aboard we made various toasts to "sunshine and mermaids" and the "adventures of the sea."

From Lunenburg we sailed through the locks of the Bras d'Or Lakes, a brackish chain of lakes in Cape Breton with hundreds of coves and islands. The fog-free conditions made it possible to see the multitude of lighthouses, beautiful anchorages and abundant wildlife. It's easy to see why this area attracts so many sailing enthusiasts. Back out into the fog and rolling seas, we then continued offshore another 62 hours to the southern coast of Newfoundland.

The next port of call was Grand Bruit, a small fishing community with extremely friendly inhabitants. Cutting the town in half is a majestic waterfall. Newfoundland had only just caught up to modern entertainment provided by electricity in the mid-'60s, so these islanders still have a real gift for storytelling and music. There was an old boathouse on the wharf, which the locals had converted into a community spot called Cram A Lot. Every evening these hardcore fishermen convened for "sundowners," their version of Happy Hour. They loved the homemade XXX Hawaiian Punch we shared with them. They had one guitar among all of them and passed it around singing hilarious, dirty drinking songs. My favorite was the little guy in the corner with Kramer hair, no teeth, playing harmonica. When he wasn't playing or drinking he was laughing hysterically at someone's joke.

From there we pressed on and continued east. The southern coast of Newfoundland sports massive, thousand-foot vertical cliff faces. Ollie nervously checked the incoming tide and his charts. With full sail on a beam reach we roared into the very narrow opening with huge vertical cliffs on either side of us. The water boiled and ripped past our tiny boat as we tried to stay in the middle of the turbulent hundred-foot-wide entrance. We called it "threading the needle." Our spirits could not have been higher as we entered the calm fjord that penetrates the core of Newfoundland. Fjords such as this one were formed when a glacier cut a u-shaped valley from the surrounding bedrock. Dotting these 10-mile-long fjords are abandoned fishing villages. This hauntingly beautiful southern coast is accessible only by boat and one of the most isolated places I've ever seen.

The region was sparsely populated by kind, thirsty fishermen who found our tiny wooden sailboat a bit odd. These self-sufficient families are true pioneers who live off the sea and moose meat. To them, a boat was simply a means for obtaining food, a commodity they were happy to share with us. The generous fishermen, eager to enjoy some of our rum and equally eager to share their own bounty, gifted us with home canned meats of moose and seal, and even the hearts of seals. Though we were on a $50,000 boat, our budget was strictly for pasta, rice and diesel, making the presents from the maritimers much appreciated. One old gent gave us a hand-line and jig and showed us where to find the cod banks. We discovered how easy it is to jig for cod. My favorite part of the day was sailing up to a new fishing pier by sunset and surprising new friends with our company and cocktails.

Day after day we moved along the coast. Our mood was way better than the weather. On the fortieth day Leif told us that he loved this adventure but would love it more if he could spend a week with his friends and family and then come back to it. This wistful admission reminded me that when you're adventuring far from home it isn't possible to just push "pause" when homesickness sets in. It takes fortitude to stay the course.

Landing on the French island of Saint-Pierre, Leif got a huge boost when he was able to realize his dream of finding big surf. A week later Ollie's dream came true as we rounded the corner to St. John's. Two weeks after that, I learned that my dream would not come true. I found out that no one climbs icebergs because it is impossible. These 10,000-year-old icebergs calf off the glaciers of Greenland, float north for two years and then slowly head south, melting in the warmer waters of southern Newfoundland. The enormous chunks of floating ice are so dense that they cannot be penetrated with ice climbing tools; one hard blow from an ice axe could potentially split a huge part of the iceberg. They are definitely not the seasonal frozen waterfalls we have back home; a scary lesson learned. I returned to the boat with no less of an adventure and a reminder that time and time again it isn't about the goal; it's about the process of chasing your dreams.

I experienced so many magical moments on this adventure: porpoise playing in phosphorescence, shortening the sails at sunset, cooking in rough weather, a wave from a humpback whale 200 feet from the boat, preparing for another night watch, trying to count the shooting stars from the Pleiades meteor shower, being amazed by how Ollie kept us safe while sailing our course in thick fog when he could barely see the bow, plenty of time to think at the tiller, watching Leif grow into more of a man, cocktail hours in tiny ports, fishing the cod banks off the southern coast, sailing along thousand-foot granite cliffs, the captain thanking me for simple chores well done, and sailing in the middle of nowhere while the boys slept. Of these many experiences, the humor and the hospitality of the Newfoundlanders are the most memorable to me.

It was time for the crew to part ways. Captain Ollie and his boat stayed in Nova Scotia. Leif and I were on our way back to the States. Leif had read the beginnings of my book, and it fuelled his adventuresome spirit. He had two months of adventure under his belt, just enough to whet his appetite. Leif wanted to hitchhike back home solo so I gave him my extra pack and he bought a tent. I figured we'd get off the peninsula together and then part ways after he had a few hitchhiking lessons.

Rosemary saw our thumbs and cardboard sign and picked us up. The fifth of 11 children, she was 82 years old and a sassy old bird who wouldn't take no for an answer when she pulled over to buy us ice cream. She told us that she had been picking up hitchhikers since she'd got her driver's license at age sixteen. We parted ways after an hour of delightful stories.

Taking awhile to get our next ride was a good opportunity to teach Leif a simple hitchhiking trick: playing the lost tourist. It is important to only approach men for a ride at a stop sign or a gas pump. And the best questions to ask are "How far is it to my destination? Are you going there?" It worked. It got us a ride to the Trans-Canadian Highway. There Leif and I parted company. He thanked me for my friendship, backpack and travel tips. I wished him good luck on his epic sail around the world. I wish I had thanked him for inspiring me to continue writing this book, but I did not think about it at the time. The last thing I shouted to him as he climbed into his next ride was, "Shine on, Leif! Shine on!"

Alyssa, Southern Newfoundland, Canada

50
Indonesia

This is the last day of 2012, and I'm finishing this last story of the book. I have just spent an amazing two months in Indonesia, the largest Muslim country and the largest archipelago in the world. It is comprised of 17,000 islands and has been an important trade region since the seventh century. Indonesia is the fourth most populated country on the planet and my favorite country of this trip.

Indonesia sports some of the best snorkeling available. The guidebook promised 10-foot manta rays, black-tipped sharks, pristine coral reefs and an infinite variety of colorful fish, and that is exactly what I got. Among other amazing things, I watched a 350-pound male orangutan swing effortlessly through the rainforest at close range. I survived a one-hour Jakarta motorcycle taxi death ride that bumped up on the sidewalks, scattering people and blindly passing the slow, smoky diesel trucks in the 105-degree heat. I stalked a poisonous Komodo dragon the length of a car.

I found the people there amazing. A great way to rub elbows with the locals is on a slow, four-day boat trip up the Sumatran coast, economy class. The decks of the rusty 300-foot ship I traveled on were absolutely overflowing with cargo and people trying to get home for the holiday season. The passengers quickly put down their sheets or grain sacks to reserve their sleeping quarters and settled in for the long journey. Men smoked and played cards in small circles. Women talked and caught up on their sleep, and hoards of excited children ran around unsupervised. Young people wandered in groups, listening to music from their phones while flirting. As the only white person and native English speaker on board, I instantly became "The English Teacher" and posed in hundreds of pictures. Indonesians are some of the nicest people on the planet! They made me feel especially welcomed.

The second night on board there was a fantastic lightning storm and by midnight it started raining heavily, forcing the open-deck passengers inside. The dirt from a thousand travelers turned into mud. Back home I would have freaked out, but I took a cue from these relaxed people and let the slow boat ride chill me out.

I had befriended the first mate Joseph, a worldly and well-read older officer who was always dressed in brilliant white. He had a son living in Los Angeles, and we had plenty to talk about. On the third morning, at sunrise, I persuaded him to let me steer the massive passenger ship for several minutes as we crossed the equator. The GPS read 000.000 latitude, and I blew the massive foghorn for at least five seconds to celebrate our crossing of the hemispheres. It was day 528 of what was to be my 775-day trip.

After finishing a second big cup of strong Javanese java with Joseph on the immaculate bridge, I headed back down to the filthy rolling ghetto. I needed a toilet. There was a long line outside all the toilets except for one, a roped-off flooded-out women's bathroom. I really needed a toilet and went for it. As I stepped over a diaper in funky ankle-deep water, the sloshing scenario reminded me of my friend Liam, a 14-year-old live aboard home-schooler, explaining the definition of "shit." He told me the old English sailing term is an acronym for "Ship High In Transit," and it refers to transporting animal fertilizer to America that had to stay high and dry because it was very smelly if it got wet. It made me laugh out loud.

I stepped into the only unlocked toilet and mounted the porcelain squatter. With every roll of the ship a new wave of dirty water sloshed around my feet. The door banged open and then shut again. The lock was broken, and I could not keep the door closed with my hand and reach the open toilet. Somehow I needed to reach a foot and a half more. I had the brilliant idea of putting my leather belt through the door handle which would give me the distance desperately needed to squat. As I pulled my belt free the camera that is always attached to my side dropped straight down the squat toilet hole. I was stunned. The door swung open, and I screamed at the top of my lungs, "Shit!" in a high-pitched voice. I quickly dropped to my knees and slid my entire bare arm down the incredibly disgusting shitty pipe. It was gone. A huge memory card filled with all my amazing pictures of Indonesia was gone! Dozens of people gathered at the roped-off bathroom entrance and stared at me in absolute horror.

Three days after the camera disaster I met Dennis, who is from Stockholm, Sweden. He had just completed a two-year English teaching stint in Korea and was soon heading home. Our rooms shared a balcony at a five-dollar-a-night traditional Batak house with an amazing view over Lake Toba. Some 75,000 years ago this was the site of a massive volcanic eruption that sent the earth into such an intense volcanic winter that it almost extinguished life on the planet! Eventually it created the world's largest volcanic crater lake. It was there that Dennis and I spent a week swimming, eating, and having great conversations.

I have been working on this book on and off for three and a half years, and am amazed at how smoothly the project has gone considering the fact that I am dyslexic and technologically incompetent. I have relied upon the help of dozens of fellow travelers just like Dennis to type out and organize my handwritten journals on their personal computers. Some of the many amazing friends and places of this project include Paddy in a castle in Wales, Matt in his little house in a Bali rice field and the Gulf Islands of British Columbia, Heidi in an old Maine farmhouse, Mardi on the west coast of Norway, Beth on *Sea Zen* in the Gulf of Mexico, Stacy in her lush Florida garden and Komi on the beaches of India. This book is a product of their generosity.

With only four hours left in the year, we have just finished writing the last story in this book. There seems no better time or occasion to give thanks in celebration.

Kevin McNally
December 31, 2012
Lake Toba, Indonesia

Countries Traveled, 1977-2012

Albania, Andorra, Argentina, Armenia, Australia, Austria, Azerbaijan, Bahamas, Bangladesh, Belgium, Belize, Benin, Bolivia, Bosnia and Herzegovina, Botswana, Brazil, Brunei, Bulgaria, Burkina Faso, Cambodia, Canada, Chile, China, Colombia, Democratic Republic of the Congo, Costa Rica, Côte d'Ivoire, Croatia, Cuba, Cyprus, Czech Republic, Denmark, Djibouti, Dominica, Ecuador, Egypt, El Salvador, Eritrea, Estonia, Ethiopia, France, Gambia, Georgia, Germany, Ghana, Greece, Guatemala, Guyana, Honduras, Hungary, Iceland, India, Indonesia, Ireland, Israel, Italy, Jamaica, Japan, Jordan, Kenya, Laos, Latvia, Lebanon, Lesotho, Liechtenstein, Lithuania, Luxembourg, Macedonia, Malawi, Malaysia, Mali, Mauritania, Mexico, Monaco, Mongolia, Montenegro, Morocco, Mozambique, Myanmar, Namibia, Nepal, Netherlands, New Zealand, Nicaragua, Niger, Norway, Pakistan, Palestine, Panama, Paraguay, Peru, Philippines, Poland, Portugal, Romania, Russia, Rwanda, Saint Lucia, Saint Vincent & the Grenadines, Senegal, Serbia, Singapore, Slovakia, Slovenia, South Africa, South Korea, Spain, Sri Lanka, Sudan, Suriname, Swaziland, Sweden, Switzerland, Syria, Tanzania, Thailand, Togo, Trinidad and Tobago, Turkey, Uganda, Ukraine, United Arab Emirates, United Kingdom, United States, Uruguay, Vatican City, Venezuela, Vietnam, Western Sahara, Zambia, Zimbabwe

Author's Note

I am in the process of writing another book about budget world travel of the 1980s. So many of today's backpackers have asked me how my generation of travelers managed without the "gifts" of internet, bank cards, guide books, and all the services provided by the present-day tourist industry. Using only paper maps and relying heavily on our intuition, years ago we constantly needed the advice of the locals and fellow travelers who were coming from the opposite direction. Rough roads, slow letters, and expensive distorted overseas phone calls allowed us to step off and embrace getting lost. The world seemed bigger and more exotic! I hope this next book will give insight into how wonderful world travel was in those days.

Excerpts from *The Open Road*
by Walt Whitman
1856

Afoot and light-hearted I take to the open road, healthy, free, the world before me, the long brown path before me leading wherever I choose. Henceforth I ask not good-fortune, I myself am good-fortune. Henceforth I whimper no more, postpone no more, need nothing. Done with indoor complaints, libraries, querulous criticisms, strong and content I travel the open road. I am larger, better than I thought. I did not know I held so much goodness. All seems beautiful to me, I can repeat over to men and women you have done such good to me I would do the same to you. I will recruit for myself and you as I go. I will scatter myself among men and women as I go. I will toss a new gladness and roughness among them. Whoever denies me it shall not trouble me. Whoever accepts me he or she shall be blessed and shall bless me. Here a great personal deed has room. Here is the test of wisdom. Wisdom is not finally tested in schools. Wisdom cannot be pass'd from one having it to another not having it. Wisdom is of the soul. Listen! I will be honest with you, I do not offer the old smooth prizes, but offer rough new prizes. These are the days that must happen to you: you shall not heap up what is call'd riches. You shall scatter with lavish hand all that you earn or achieve. Allons! The road is before us! It is safe, I have tried it, my own feet have tried it well, be not detain'd! Let the paper remain on the desk unwritten, and the book on the shelf unopen'd! Let the tools remain in the workshop! Let the money remain unearn'd! Let the school stand! Mind not the cry of the teacher! Let the preacher preach in his pulpit! Let the lawyer plead in the court, and the judge expound the law. Camerado, I give you my hand! I give you my love more precious than money, I give you myself before preaching or law; will you give me yourself? Will you come travel with me?

Our Music

While my mother prepared dinner and my father watched the graphic death toll of the Vietnam War on our small black-and-white television in the living room, down in the basement we spun vinyl records and sang songs of peace, love and unity.

I was deeply influenced by the psychedelic music of my youth and the songs promoting the freedom of the open road. On the next few pages are snippets from some of those influential traveling songs.

Eagles
Take It Easy, 1972

Well, I'm a standing on a corner
In Winslow, Arizona
And such a fine sight to see
It's a girl, my Lord, in a flatbed Ford
slowin' down to take a look at me
Come on, baby, don't say maybe
I gotta know if your sweet love is
Gonna save me
We may lose or we may win
Though we will never be here again
so open up, I'm climbin' in,
so take it easy

Creedence Clearwater Revival
Proud Mary, 1969

Left a good job in the city
Workin' for the man every night and day
And I never lost one minute of sleepin'
Worryin' 'bout the way things might have been

Cleaned a lot of plates in Memphis
Pumped a lot of 'pane down in New Orleans
But I never saw the good side of the city
'Til I hitched a ride on a river boat queen

If you come down to the river
Bet you gonna find some people who live
You don't have to worry 'cause you have no money
People on the river are happy to give

———————

Janis Joplin
Me and Bobby Magee, 1971

Busted flat in Baton Rouge
Waitin' for a train
And I's feelin' near as faded as my jeans
Bobby thumbed a diesel down
Just before it rained
It rode us all the way into New Orleans

Freedom's just another word for nothin' left to lose.

Crosby, Stills & Nash
Wooden Ships, 1969

And it's a fair wind
Blowin' warm out of the south over my shoulder
Guess I'll set a course and go

If you smile at me I will understand
'Cause that is something
Everybody everywhere does in the same language

———————

Cat Stevens
Peace Train, 1971

Get your bags together,
go bring your good friends too
Cause it's getting nearer,
it soon will be with you

Now come and join the living,
it's not so far from you
And it's getting nearer,
soon it will all be true

Now I've been crying lately,
thinking about the world as it is
Why must we go on hating,
why can't we live in bliss

'Cause out on the edge of darkness,
there rides a peace train
Oh peace train take this country,
come take me home again.

James Taylor
Sweet Baby James, 1970

Now the first of December was covered with snow
And so was the turnpike from Stockbridge to Boston. Though the
Berkshires seemed dreamlike on account of that frosting, with ten miles
behind me and
ten thousand more to go.

———————

Cat Stevens
Miles From Nowhere, 1970

Miles from nowhere
I guess I'll take my time
Oh yeah, to reach there
Look up at the mountain
I have to climb
Oh yeah, to reach there.
Lord my body has been a good friend
But I won't need it when I reach the end
Miles from nowhere
Guess I'll take my time
Oh yeah, to reach there

The Beatles
Let It Be, 1970

When I find myself in times of trouble
Mother Mary comes to me
Speaking words of wisdom, let it be
And in my hour of darkness
She is standing right in front of me
Speaking words of wisdom, let it be

And when the brokenhearted people
Living in the world agree
There will be an answer, let it be
For though they may be parted
There is still a chance that they will see
There will be an answer, let it be

Whisper words of wisdom, let it be
And when the night is cloudy
There is still a light that shines on me
Shine on until tomorrow, let it be
I wake up to the sound of music,
Mother Mary comes to me
Speaking words of wisdom, let it be

Grateful Dead
Ripple, 1970

If my words did glow with the gold of sunshine
And my tunes were played on the harp unstrung,
Would you hear my voice come through the music?
Would you hold it near as it were your own?

It's a hand-me-down, the thoughts are broken,
Perhaps they're better left unsung.
I don't know, don't really care
Let there be songs to fill the air.

Ripple in still water,
When there is no pebble tossed,
Nor wind to blow.

Reach out your hand if your cup be empty,
If your cup is full, may it be again,
Let it be known there is a fountain,
That was not made by the hands of men.

There is a road, no simple highway,
Between the dawn and the dark of night,
And if you go, no one may follow,
That path is for your steps alone.

You, who choose to lead, must follow
But if you fall, you fall alone.
If you should stand, then who's to guide you?
If I knew the way, I would take you home.

Jim Croce
I Got a Name, 1973

Like the pine trees lining the winding road
I got a name, I got a name
Like the singing bird and the croaking toad
I got a name, I got a name
And I carry it with me like my daddy did
But I'm living the dream that he kept hid

Moving me down the highway
Rolling me down the highway
Moving ahead so life won't pass me by

Like the north wind whistling down the sky
I've got a song, I've got a song
Like the whippoorwill and the baby's cry
I've got a song, I've got a song
And I carry it with me and I sing it loud
If it gets me nowhere, I go there proud
And I'm gonna go there free

Like the fool I am and I'll always be
I've got a dream, I've got a dream
They can change their minds but they can't change me
I've got a dream, I've got a dream
Well, I know I can share it if you want me to
If you're going my way, I'll go with you

Moving me down the highway
Rolling me down the highway
Moving ahead so life won't pass me by

Crosby, Stills & Nash
Marrakesh Express, 1969

Looking at the world through the sunset in your eyes
Traveling the train through clear Moroccan skies

Steppenwolf
Born to Be Wild, 1968

Get your motor runnin'. Head out on the highway.
Lookin' for adventure and whatever comes our way.
Yeah Darlin' go make it happen. Take the world in a love embrace.
Fire all of your guns at once and explode into space.

I like smoke and lightning, heavy metal thunder.
Racin' with the wind and the feelin' that I'm under.
Yeah Darlin' go make it happen. Take the world in a love embrace.

Like a true nature's child, We were born, born to be wild
We can climb so high I never wanna die.

Born to be wild.

Acknowledgments

I thank my friends, family and my traveling companions from all over the world. Your English skills and computers made this book possible.

A special thank-you to my mother, Anne McNally, my father, Gene, my brother E.J. and his daughter Emma, my brother Chris, my sister Karen Nelson, Komi Ayumi, Matt Bigham, Leslie Case, Christine Christianson, Bonnie Farrell, Tom Froehle, Beth Griffin, Mardi Kristin Iversen, Greg Jones, Dennis Lamberg, Donna Lemmon, Heidi Lewis, David Leveille, John Mayhew, cover: Margaret O'Rourke, Dave Paddy, Jodi Patterson, Stacy Radford, Yoshihava Takeshi, Wen Chin Ter, and Marco Werman.

Road angels: the Allens, the Arsenaults, Mary Ashton, the Bendoskis, Bill Bixby, the Bruners, the Doyles, Suzanne Evans, the Giblin Clan, the Griffin families, Sue Haynes, Nancy Heroux, Elizabeth Kenyan, the Krouses, Bruce McIlvain, the McNally clan, the Nelsons, the Parkers, Elsa Pons, Floyd Radford, Tim Rodd, Eileen Seaberg, the Smiths, the Snyders, Jay Southgate, Tom Tibbets, Petra Weinman, and to the countless others this old guy has forgotten to include.

I have journeyed the limits of this world,
Seen magical things and met many people,
And I find that across the four oceans
All men are brothers.

-Unknown Ancient Mariner

Give this book a review on Amazon.com
and pass it on to a friend. Thanks. Shine on!

-Kevin